THE PSYCHOLOGY OF WELFARE

FÉLIX VARELA COLLECTION # 68

EDICIONES UNIVERSAL, Miami, Florida, 2024

JORGE SALAZAR-CARRILLO

THE PSYCHOLOGY OF WELFARE

..-EDICIONES UNIVERSAL

INDEX

ACKNOWLEDGMENTS

This book is dedicated to the posthumous memory of Father Juan B. Cortes, Ph. D., member of the Order of the Company of Jesus (Jesuits), and a distinguished member of the religious and intellectual circles in his native city of Alicante, Spain. After obtaining his Ph..D. in Psychology at Harvard University, Father Cortés joined the Department of Psychology at Georgetown University eventually becoming its chairman. Our paths crossed when the Brookings Institution, where I was a Senior Fellow, allowed me to teach part-time at Georgetown University, as a Professorial Lecturer in the Department of Economics. This book reflects the exchanges we had over the years on the topics of psychological well-being and economic welfare at the individual level.

I also wish to express my gratitude to Ramón Boza, M.D., with whom these topics were discussed over the years, when he was a professor of psychiatry in Baltimore, Maryland and at the University of Miami, Miami, Florida. I am grateful as well to Father José Pascual Burgess, Sch.P., who read the manuscript and provided useful suggestions, and to Daniel Murgo, Ph.D., whose varied support was constant throughout the revisions. They remain blameless for any flaws that may remain in this essay.

Jorge Salazar-Carrillo

I

INTRODUCTION

A) Objectives of the Book

We will strive to provide a synthesis that will help the reader attain psychological and animic welfare from reading this book. It has always seemed to us that economic welfare is insufficient. In fact, it may even be counterproductive. After many centuries of examining and experiencing material well-being, it has been found wanting when considered from the perspective of interior fulfillment. This finding applies not only to individuals, but to families, groups, cities, regions, and countries.

It is only through internal contentment that psychological welfare can be achieved. However, in the substantial majority of circumstances, if we can defray our pursuits of material goods, and concentrate on improving our psyche, we will fail as well, unless we are willing to open ourselves as well to the realm of spirituality. Philosophy and beliefs seem to be more fulfilling than economics, and as essential as psychology, in providing the leads that lead to true welfare. Certainly, economic pursuits, but psychological objectives in most cases, as well, are too direct and individualistic to lead to psychic and spiritual contentment, given that this seems to be indissolubly tied to orienting one's life to others rather than to self.

Only philosophy and theology strive to seriously understand faith which appears to be comprehensible by definition. Economics only deals with self-confidence indirectly; psychology handles it directly. But this is only one of the attributes of faith. Only the former disciplines confront it. Yet, in order to understand psychological and animic welfare fully, it is essential to examine its role in guiding human behavior. A well-known aphorism states that *knowledge will*

9

set you free (of the Greek philosophical maxim: *know thyself*), but in order to think and learn it is necessary to have faith (*credo ut intelligem*), which makes it the basis of all human achievements. It is in spiritual pursuits that we encounter faith, and once it has been found, it proves to be a key to increased spirituality. Throughout the pages of this book, we will stress that this is the essential attribute required for well-being. And the various types and mechanisms explained and recommended for human welfare will be solidly based on the cornerstone of faith.

B) Nature of the Book

To explain the concept of psychological and animic welfare, a spiritual approach is essential. However, we will find supporting elements in thought, introspection, and readings, in order to attain this objective. Yet, we will eventually conclude the latter on their own are not promising approaches, unless they are primed in spiritual faith and self-confidence.

Reading and pondering alone are not to be trusted, given the well-known scientific principle that nothing can be proven. Introspective reasoning is limited by the natural tendencies towards emotional bias, hidden assumptions and self-ego reinforcement. Thinking tends to become excessive, once confronted with the essential truth that humanity cannot fully explain the essence of even the simplest things in life. Being aware of these basic principles of human knowledge, many of the psychological traps which befall us in trying to understand life, can be successfully avoided. In the end, living a successful animic and psychological existence is like pursuing an art, as very artfully Andre Maurois stressed in his famous book *The Art of Living*.[1] Without faith and spirituality, attempting to obtain psychological and animic (or spiritual) well-being by being over-conscious about life, and attempting to fully understand it, can lead us to dysfunctionality.

---

[1] Likewise, Lin Yutang's, *The Importance of Living*.

In this essay our approach will be holistic. We will use all the cognitive elements at our disposal, but they will be fully anchored on faith[2] and spirituality, assured of the contributions that intuition and emotion provide. This will allow the attainment of our objectives, and to ensure their fulfilling application by the readers.

---

[2] From which faith in ourselves is derived, based on the *primus movens* of Saint Thomas Aquinas, God himself.

II

THE MEANING OF LIFE

A) The Mystery

As in an enormous spaceship (Spaceship Earth) in the universe, we human bengs traverse at dizzying speed, this poorly known medium. Those that have devoted the most time and effort to understanding and deciphering these circumstances have concluded that very little is known with certainty. Hypotheses and theories abound, but proofs are not forthcoming. We have learned about the interactions among certain things, but this knowledge has only been conductive to a better utilization of what our world is made of, but not to a real understanding of their substance.

We know we circle our Sun, the source of all the energy on the Earth, as if we were egotistically it. But we are not fully aware of how our planetary system traverses within the Milky Way galaxy, and how the latter circles about an axis (seemingly a black hole), while all this traverses an almost infinite cosmos.

Our limitations, however, do not diminish the intensity of our questioning or the acuteness of our analysis: we need to know as much in order to live. Inside of us, there is an imminent curiosity, and our strongest desires are of a trascendental nature. What and who are we? What is our purpose? Where do we come from and why?[3] And after dying, do we have a destiny? An ephemeral existence is not acceptable to us. There has to be a reason behind all this. It is senseless to be prisoners in our bodies, clustered in this spaceship, with a limited projection within the immense universe.

---

[3] Debating, although it may seem incredible, these issues, lost in the mountains of southern Mexico, with descendants of the Mayan race, this response was received from an indigenous person: "We are, because if we are not, what the hell are we for?

A few have other means than reasoning for deciphering these questions; yet we must take for granted that our grey cerebral matter is as scarce and deficient as everything else in our Spaceship Earth. Moreover, our limited intelligence must concentrate in solving our basic existential needs. Our intellectual capabilities end up being applied to solving the mundane problems to which we tie our welfare, trying to attain the greatest satisfaction from the limited availability of goods we unravel from nature. Thus, our day-to-day objectives end up constraining our mental gifts, not allowing them to be devoted to transcendental questions. And it even greatly deviates the devotion of those who are gifted with intuitive and mystical from confronting their attention to pondering the essential questions.

B) Pondering: The Universe and the Molecule

Of those that have used reason and logic[4] to unwind the script of human existence, the ones that have profited the most from their efforts have studied the largest and the smallest. Those that have looked into the sub-atomic particles, armed by quantum theory, and the ones that have examined the largest bodies of the universe from the vantage points of cosmology and astrophysics. The latter have concluded that the myriads of galaxies are driven by a complex but deterministic set of principles, whether they can be perceived or not by our senses[5]. The former considered that at least the sub-atoms would seem to be ruled by the probabilities of game theory and is not deterministic.

---

[4]   The letter began with Aristotle, continuing with Saint Augustine and Saint Thomas Aquinas. The norms that these thinkers developed are still applied.

[5]   The most distinguished exponent of this approach was Albert Einstein who wrote: "*Gott würfelt nicht!*" This dictum expresses disbelief that God does not leave the matter of our universe to chance. The ordered creation we perceive is not only based on the various dimensions (perceived or met) of a logic, mathematical type, including time as one of the mystics as Saint Augustine pointed out centuries ago and now eminent cosmologists recognize.

The quantum theorists have prevailed over time, as their main tenet, the uncertainty principle postulated by Werner Heisenberg, establishing that in the infinitesimal sub-atomic world of particles, it practically is impossible to determine with certainty, both the position and the movement o of atomic and sub-atomic particles. This principle seemed to influence the knowledge of creation, since it also established that the experimenter exerts an influence over the observed reality. When the uncertainty principle and its corollary are applied to electrons or photons, it is found that these dominant particles of energy can be considered to have the generality of ubiquity, occupying more than one position in space at the same time. Furthermore, they seem to be found in the position or place expected by the experimenter. From which it can be deduced that anthropocentrism is the phenomenon prevailing in the universe, allowing human beings to perceive its existence.

After these considerations, it is not difficult to conclude that the spiritual realm provides the only satisfactory dimension. Material things cannot be explained with certitude, which is what would be expected from tangible objects, while spiritual concepts do not require logical and scientific proof, and only a belief in faith. That is, an animic convincement which emanates from the spirit (and for which reasoning is only a support), fundamentally flowing from imminent interior forces forming what is accepted. Therefore, the north star in our journey to emerge from Plato's dark cavern, which is the material reality, is to maintain a holistically comprehensive approach, illumined by transcendental inspiration, which is the only one that could lead us into a self-journey.

C) The Spirit, the Mind, and the Body

It is well known that, although different and distinct, there are infinite indentations between mind and body. Psychiatrists and psychologists have established the connections which have been found to be close, between thoughts, emotions, beliefs, and other mental manifestations, and the behavior of the body. These professionals have also concluded that corporal physiology in turn influences mental states and their manifestations. Less researched has been the interconnection of mind and body with the spirit that inhabits every human being. Yet many philosophers, theologians and even some members of the professions just listed above, have determined that religiosity, and the relationships of human beings with themselves, suppressed through their self-judgments, bring about straight-forward reactions in their minds and bodies. Thus, the well-known old dictum should be transformed into "*mens et anima sanae in corpore sano.*"

We could define the human being in its entirety as composed of these parts: spirit, mind and body.[6] If one of these is lacking, the integrity of man could not be defined. These three components are necessary and sufficient to constitute a whole human being.

However, if we had to choose in terms of their importance to humanity, primacy would have to go to the spirit. The approximately 20,000 years of historical records during the neolithic period show a constant force that inspired and directed human beings: religious spirituality. The essential drive of the spirit is what drives the actions of mind and body. If man is not convinced that it can use its mental intelligence or utilize its corporal senses (*credo ut intelligem*), little can be accomplished.

D) Lieben und Arbeiten

Life could be extremely complicated if we do not allow the spirit to guide our minds and bodies. In our existence we are continuously confronting real or imaginary dangers. Even those that are real require that we define them as such through mental processes similar to imagination. Only in this fashion can we react to them, even though

---

[6] Unfortunately, the rationalism of Descartes put the spirit aside, placing it in the pineal body. Eventually creating much confusion in psychiatry and psychology but attempting to separate spirituality from the fully integrated human being. In delineating my different approach, it is preferable to me *to summereo cogito,* instead of the famous Cartesian one: *cogito ergo sum.*

we end up ignoring them, when not constituting real threats. It is here that the spirit provides essential guidance.

If we are to examine a minimizable sliver of the trillions of thoughts that on a daily basis, pass through our minds (and this is a conservative estimate), whether consciously, subconsciously or unconsciously, it would be impossible to accomplish anything.[7] Particularly when a good portion of them brings us worry. This is why early in life, with the help of our parents and close adults, we develop an instinctively discerning skill that allows us to dètermine which of these to give attention to. This intuitive leap of faith that allows us to proceed with our life without endless pondering, is directed by our spirit.

How prodigious is this accomplishment! If our mental stimuli are analyzed, it can be concluded that as pointed out earlier, they are combinations of thoughts, emotions, imagery and bodily reactions, immersed in a background of noise.[8] Thus, to live a healthy life of mind and body, it is essential to concentrate in the essence and belief that emanate from our spirit, without allowing them to be confused or perturbed by our unending mental elucidations.

Sigmund Freud, without understanding much about spirituality, (the little that he knew was incorporated in his concept of a weak super ego), became aware that the essence of life is love and work (Lieben und Arbeiten). Only if we lead our life formatted in the real and positive things and guided by the faith and intuition of the spirit, can we avoid falling prey to the unimportant and impertinent thoughts and impulses that our mind and to a lesser degree, our body, generate.

---

[7] A computer that processes simultaneously five billion instructions per second, is equivalent to the operations undertaken by the brain of a child.

[8] It is very difficult to become aware of this list of factors that exemplifies the prodigious simultaneity of our tridimensional essence: spirit, mind, and body. It is illustrative to recall that Beethoven sometimes complained about the unstoppable music that his brain continuously and spontaneously generated. Ramón Boza, M.D. provided an illustrative example of this interaction where he referred to what occurred to the famous composer, Shostakovich during the siege of Leningrad that took place during the Second World War. He was hit by a kernel in the head and afterwards, depending on how he moved, his brain would generate melodies. Of course, he never wanted to extract the piece of metal from his head.

The latter are activisms generated from a strictly ani mediatic past like the flight or fight syndrome, which are useful because they make us aware of dangers, but that should be filtered through our spirits, which is where the essence of our lives reside: love and work.

E) Transcendental Wishes for Eternal Rest

Who am I? Where am I? These questions resonate now and then in the conscience of every living person. The only answer that can be given requires faith, which stems from the spirit. Our intellect, guided by science, is continually striving unsuccessfully to provide definitive answers. As scientists we are aware that these will never be definitive, because there are no eternal proofs, but best explanations that are widely accepted at any given time. The evolution of science provides the most acceptable explanations at any given moment of time, but not the final and definitive ones. This is the best that scientific laws can attain. Explanations, frequently called scientific laws. These explanations can be shown to be patently weak, when transcendental questions are confronted, like those with which this paragraph began. At that juncture, science refers us to metaphysics, which addresses the fundamental causes of our existence.

Moreover, when such deep questions are considered, our interior forces remit us to the supernatural for answers. Of the three essential components of humanity, intellect, mind and spirit, it is the latter that can open a window to the supernatural, and its operation is based on faith. We have an immanent awareness that our destiny is not restricted to optimistically, a century of wandering universe. That we were created and placed within the rest of creation with a purpose. Our intuition suggests this to be the case.

Our worldly endeavors must be guided by the understanding that it is the life of the spirit that provides the time path that should be followed, and that our material circumstances can only partially provide for our total fulfillment, that only will occur at the end of our worldly existence and the new horizons that are opened at that moment.[9] If we are cognizant that this is truly our destiny, nothing could frighten us during our mundane existence. Thus, the two questions with which this section begins are answered, although cognizant that completely and fully, as without the requirement of faith, they will only be completely understood in the spiritual life that awaits us.

F) The Art of Living

Our life on this Earth should not be questioned or analyzed. Living is not to be analyzed, but rather experienced. If we concentrate on explanations, sight is lost of our time destiny, and the simplest things become complicated. We give weight to the most ephemeral questions and become embroiled in the vacuous odyssey of explaining our own lives to ourselves, like the foolish scientists trying to fully understand nature. But even worse, because we are object and subject of the experiment, and thus our geniuses go out the window. This is why those who have attained fulfillment in life have experienced it through the awareness of the spirit, and the assuredness of faith.

Life should be an imminent happening during which we accomplish our journey guided by a transcendental destiny. This translates into actions that are the intuitive expressions of our essence, which by definition cannot be questioned. We have been created by God with qualities that are above our apparent limitations. This is why Jesus, while preparing the apostles for preaching, suggested to them that they not worry beforehand about what they would say, but rather to follow their heart (spirit). Likewise, this explains the deep beliefs of Saint Paul when he wrote: "For I can do all things through Christ, who strengthens me."[10] It comes without saying that it is through the Spirit of Jesus and the Father, that this becomes possible, because this is the basis of creation.

---

[9] As Saint Paul wrote, eyes have not seen, or ears have heard, what God has reserved for us at this juncture.

[10] Philippians 4:13 13

If we understand the simplicity of our earthly peregrination, others should never be needed to interpret our remittance, because it would understand intuitively through the life of the spirit. How many hours of psychotherapy would be unneeded if we understood, as the Spanish poet Antonio Machado wrote: "There is no road, rather we make it as we walk"? And while we are ambulating, spiritual faith is our walking cane.

G) Inner Direction

Most of the problems of those that question the difficulties of material life emerge from lack of self-respect and self-esteem. These people do not understand how important it is to find the compass within us, and do not feel worthy. Would they be surprised to learn that this happens when they consider themselves just matter? They clearly see that the latter is evanescent, imperfect, and subject to deterioration. If we only understand ourselves as a material body, and even in terms of electric and chemical reactions in our brain, how could self-deprecation be avoided. It is the animic and spiritual life, which is based on faith, which can provide a way out of the dilemma.

The debate between philosophers and thoughtful persons regarding the ideas of two outstanding thinkers within this Christian thought, Saint Augustine, and Saint Anselm, is well known. These two extraordinary minds debated and disagreed whether faith or reason would have precedence in attaining knowledge, acknowledging of course that both of them are its fundamental components.[11] Whichever comes first, it is necessary to underline that without faith, you cannot attain knowledge, because its essential ingredient is to be convinced that one

---

[11] *"Credo ut intelligem"* according to Saint Augustine. Or *"intelligem at credem"* following Saint Anselm.

can apply reason, and that other human beings have accomplished it before.[12]

Self-confidence emanates from faith, and our own deliberations (which must be well-founded in knowledge) emerge from our conclusions. The latter requires that we have self-confidence, and consequently that we know how to use our discernment as our interior guiding compass.

Our Creator has given us free will, dignifying Himself and ourselves, by allowing us to determine, through our own criteria, how we would pursue our existence. This inner direction is the essential compass for knowing and conducting ourselves in the world. His is the *sine qua non* of our existence, because not being aware of the worldly things we could not survive. If we do not believe (have faith) in ourselves, how could we know and believe in the matter outside ourselves? We cannot give what we do not have. We must begin by having faith in ourselves so that we can then extend to all things that exist outside ourselves. Those that must be believed and known to exist.

H) Outward Orientation

But even though the compass in our human life must be found within ourselves, for truly whole self-realization humans must direct their actions to satisfying the needs of those around them. The goal that makes man complete is to love and live for the other, and not egotistically for himself. This would seem to contradict the previous section, but in reality, is just the opposite. To understand and successfully accomplish things in the world, we should follow our own internal guidance, but always in the ways that would lead us to satisfying the needs of our neighbors. To concentrate on ourselves as the ultimate goal, leads to unhappiness. Only by serving others will we attain self-satisfaction.

---

[12] Blaise Pascal expressed that: "Le couer a ses raisons, que la raison ne connait pas." And an anonymous one, that we cannot know anything, we can only believe it or not.

Jesus Christ, the perfect human being, lived the most fulfilling life imaginable, by serving others. He was sanctified by the Creator not only for our redemption, but to guide us away from our original sin: egocentrism. Jesus lived totally compenetrated with his Father's design, as his only Son. From the time when He established his life of love of neighbor as his central message, all those that have asked themselves about the full realization of the human being, have found it in lovingly serving their fellow men. Psychology and psychiatry in contemporary times offer us some advice in focusing on other orientations.

To love and to serve the other are the streaks of life that lead us to internal peace. To the contrary, self-concentration leads us to a sickly over-awareness of ourselves, breeding continuous soliloquies of self-worry, from which we can never exit satisfactorily. Being self-centered is surely a prescription for unhappiness. *A contrario sensu*, when we give of ourselves to others, we receive from them, and ourselves, the highest genuine service and love that could be found in this world. This is why in *A Cour in Miracles* it is stated that love and peace we give to ourselves.[13]

I) Summarizing

In synthesis, the mysteries of the universe, of the molecules, of our being, of the spirit, etc., can only be unraveled through living itself. And lives should be internally directed by our free will, but should be oriented towards our fellow human beings. In this equilibrated existence, we will find the answers to all questions, not in a philosophic and scientific fashion, but in a subconscious and immanent manner. Our guides in this journey should be our faith and our spirit, which should provide the guiding posts for our navigational instruments, our mind and intelligence, which must be directed toward a life filled with love of neighbor (*caritas vincit omnia*)

---

[13] *Foundation for Inner Peace*, mentioned in Gerald G. Jampolsky, M.D., *Love is Letting Go of Fear*, Bantam Books, New York, 1985..

The previous phase in Latin hides a great secret, that we will only understand fully by totally understanding the mystery of life offered to charity or love. It is really by loving others that we will realize the love standing others, that we shall understand ourselves.[14] For this is obtained not only by meditation and contemplation of God, but by doing, especially, the good deeds. The veil of ignorance is not opened wide because of introspection and internal purification, but through the indirect process of directing our lives to the love of others. Happiness or nirvana is a corollary of our living because it is through our neighbor ("el prójimo" in Spanish), that we attain total knowledge, including that of ourselves, for which it is essential to attain the interior peace that is a gift of our love.

---

[14]   Nobody gives what it does not have, is an old Roman aphorism. Previously we shed a phrase attributed to Lao-Tse, founder of Daoism (or Taoism): "Those that look inwardly do not illuminate." Closer to our day (in the twentieth century), the famous psychiatrist Carl Jung, a disciple of Sigmund Freud, that eventually disagreed with him, stated that only if we give it, can we know we have it. For a more comprehensive vision see the Encyclical by Pope Benedict XVI, *Deus Caritas Est.*

III

BEHAVIOR: NATURE OR NURTURE?

A) Human Potential

Those that study an infants life in her mother's womb marvel at how much it resembles a born child. It is increasingly clear that the fetus constitutes an independent being, even though it requires his maternal body for subsistence. However, after birth, this "dependency" continues,[15] being critical for a number of years. Thus, it would seem evident that a substantial part of behavior is instinctive, defined in the initial moments of conception.

The recently born child also shows a startling ability to define his own active space. Most of his behavior is genetically determined, as if his ancestors' left marks in his cells, to guide during the early years of his existence. In fact, we now know that infants develop their own language in an innate fashion, and they seem to be "speaking in tongues" before they reach the age of three. From then on, they use a language well called motherly, and their own original one falls by the wayside.

While this imminent knowledge determines most of the early-child behavior, we know that these small human beings are also continuously absorbing knowledge at this time. The conditioning of the future women or men takes place almost from life's beginning in the mother's womb, because some senses are present in the fetus, especially the "sixth sense." All of it begins to leave an imprint on this genetically defined primordial existence.

---

[15] Some zoologists consider that we never "are" complete, calling this phenomenon neoteny. This information was given to me by psychiatrist Ramón Boza.

B) Human Limitations

While the beginning of life offers to human beings these innate or learned opportunities for an amazing development of their life, some limitations are also wired in from birth in their body, character, and personality. Their genetic code could limit achievement through sickness or abnormalities. But all are afflicted, in a major or minor way, by psychological problems that will accompany them during part or all of their lives.

Observing babies, their afflictions are easily perceived. Even fetuses provide signs of stress particularly when their mother's labor at childbirth becomes complicated. After being born signs of anxiety can be readily observed during the early years of their existence. A lingering personal remembrance is that of an infant that would calm itself by self-curling its hair in a repeated fashion. From the earliest in our existence, we experience fright and anguish, and calm ourselves of these emotions, or cry out for others to provide comfort. The impressionability and suggestive ability of human beings is apparent from a very early age.

Later, more sophisticated ways to combat our frailties are developed, like repressing our disagreeable experiences. Likewise, uncertain about the future, we focus our immediate concerns on present satisfaction, developing a myopic vision of human life.

C) Ensuring positive net results

In order to attain our objectives and the potential satisfactions that life can provide, it is essential to confront our traits without repressions, anxieties, or frights. It is important to understand that God has provided us with the capability of finding solutions to problems. Some prefer to call these the "least bad" for the problem at hand. It is preferable to label them, at the end of the probe, as "the best." But still more important is to recognize that human beings tend to normally concentrate on the problem, and not on the solution.

However, another inimical tendency of humans is the denial of the problems that confront us. Doing this assures us of continued martyrdom. This trait of human nature can become so complicated that it can develop into a psychological illness called cognitive dissonance. Those that are afflicted by this common malady perceive and understand reality, but they interpret it in a way that clouds or alters its truthful meaning, leading them to derive false conclusions from the facts. In this context we must be remindful of the words of Jesus Christ: "only the truth will set you free."

Another grave defect of human beings is their tendency towards emotional behavior, which is generally presently related to the just described cognitive dissonance. Cognitive psychologists, beginning with Albert Ellis, have described how we react to stimuli (actions) simplifying them through schemes known as ABC. It starts with stimulus that the mind perceives (A). This is followed by a thought or cognition (belief) (B) that evaluates it; it then ends in an emotional reaction, an action or a combination of the two (consequence) (C). Unfortunately, human nature has a tendency to allow in stage (B) the entering of irrational thoughts or beliefs that influence us (also called negative, because of the results they produce) resulting in emotional reactions and/or harmful actions.

D) Differences with Animal Instincts

As part of the animal kingdom, we share a similar genetic composition with other animals. Yet, our intrinsic capabilities separate us from the rest. Only humans have soul, spirit, and self-awareness. The others, at most, have an instinctive brain that can only be trained with difficulty. This means that for their purposes and satisfactions, they are fundamentally programmed by instinct. That is, they lack conscience and consciousness.

Our higher intellectual and spiritual powers come accompanied by free will and responsibilities. We are not pre-programmed and as a result we are responsible for our actions, and the worries that they entail. Our reactions to stimuli in the previously refined stage (B) are not instintive, and thus, we do not remain impassive or unemotional to them. We are contrastingly conscious of our own decision powers and that makes humans prone to the psychological afflictions mentioned at the end of the previous section.

Even though human beings are also driven by instinctive forces, these are much more subdued, because of acculturation and the presence of free will. While our Freudian super-egos drive our conscience to a continuous emulation, whether conscious or unconscious, of our actions, and even our thoughts. As a result, human beings are prone to doubts and psychological considerations, that contrast with the relative impassiveness of the rest of the animals, although the latter can also experience simple and instinctive emotions.

E) Instinct, Intuition and Reason

In the recent past, the contribution of genetic and biological factors in human behavior has been reevaluated, leading to the conclusion that they are preponderant. Those influences that are contributed through the family by the learned behavior that results from the customs, habits, traditions and decisions of the parents, and their influence over infant and child, are now considered of secondary importance. It is more nature than nurture. Many of the things that humans do are instinctive, and take their course without the involvement of our will. Humans are programmed for locomotion, conversation, gregariousness, etc. Our language, thoughts, feelings, and other basic characteristics of homo sapiens, are intrinsic to huma nature. They are inscribed in our brains like the reflexive automatic activities involved in respiration and the beating of the heart. Thus, when the pre-Socratic Greek philosophers, known as the sophists would ask and ponder how humans walked, the cynical philosopher Diogenes would locomote, and would say that was the answer to the question. These matters were defined by being human, and were not subject to philosophical inquiries.

From the moment of conception, we are characterized by the dichotomy between intuition and reason. Somehow human beings are capable of reaching a conclusion instantaneously, without following an orderly process of step-by-step reasoning. But they can as well follow the latter rational steps, applying logic and syllogisms. The often-used expression of using common sense, which is akin to one of the senses that humanity has by nature and definition, applies to obtaining conclusions by simple and straightforward reasoning. This seems to be the most widely used way for humans to understand matters and appears to be the essence of our rationality (the sense that we have in common). But realistically, as humans tend to mix reason with emotion, it could also be stated that common sense is the least common of all senses. Intuition and reasoning, and their interactions with emotion, constitute the innate ways which we determine our actions and conduct, Although the experience and training that we acquire by living, will help to modulate and perfect these positive forces, improving our outcomes, by appropriately adjusting them to the circumstances.

F) The basic faith required for living.

As has been previously established, the primordial requirement for human accomplishment is faith. The famous dichotomy of "fides queren intellectum or intellectum querens fidem" is in reality, false. Intelligence must be based on faith. From an early age trust is the basis of knowledge. That explains how completely we believe and learn from our teachers in primary school, without their demonstration of any historical or geographical fact. In high school, all science and mathematics believed without proof by the students. It is only at the college level that they finally reveal the secret that nothing can really be proven. We cannot even prove to ourselves, without genetic testing, that our parents really are who we believe. It can now be understood how important was the saying of our kindergarten teachers when they implored us to learn the arithmetic tables and the letters and syllables, that we could really understand them, notwithstanding our doubts given by the initial difficulties. And convinced by pristine and infantile faith, we plowed forwards, mastering the insecurities innate in human beings.

Deep down it is necessary to assume we can undertake the things we do in order to accomplish them. And such faith permeates the use of our mind, and all of our learning, because if we doubt, as Peter and the other Apostles, tears chided for lack of faith, we will not be able to achieve our potential. Of course, faith is a necessary but not a sufficient condition for everything, because training and repetition are also required). Therefore, we may conclude that the scaffold of our knowledge is in the end not different from our religious beliefs, with self-confidence being a key factor. We can only give what we have.

In the final instance, self-confidence is the keystone of the whole rational edifice of beliefs that we must build. If this is not present, nothing can be believed since we cannot give what we do not have. As much as we believe in something, it is because we trust in ourselves, and by extension we become capable of believing in other matters. This is why from childhood our parents ingrained us (generally by instinct) with self-confidence.

Nonetheless, if we examine our behavior in infancy, we can clearly induce that our self-confidence[16] is innate. Therefore, to believe, or to have faith, is an intrinsic quality of humanity, and is the principal instrument at our disposal for learning precisely. Yet, early in infancy, as self-awareness begins, and the complex mind develops discriminating and dubious, it is necessary for our parents and early teachers to reassure us of that early faith in ourselves.

G) Handed-Down Knowledge

At any given moment in the history of humanity, we find that at least 95 percent of existing knowledge has been handed down by previous generations. The most convincing proof of this statement is provided by philosophy. How much more have we added to this field of study since the Greek philosophers? Even though the recent techno-

---

[16]   That it is granted by divine omnipotence.

logical advances appear impressive, if we ponder a bit, it can be concluded that when compared with the accumulation of previous knowledge, we are only slowly developing the derivations of the theories of relativity and quantum mechanics that were developed about one hundred years ago.

From generation to generation, in spaces of time defined by quarter-centuries, we keep building our intellectual capital in all our branches of knowledge, at a minimal pace. This can also be said of the branch of philosophy comprising human behavior, and what Andre Maurois called the art of living. In general, our infant years with effort and care, and this can be attained with relative ease if we persist (which curiously is easier to do when we become older) it will be found that our ancestors continuously were handing to us kernels of wisdom. These were easily and faithfully absorbed as if we were receptors of hormonal agents. Acquired culture nurtured our being through the little understood symbiosis of faith and intelligence. Or correspondingly, our bodies and minds interacted based on total faith that what our parents told us would lead us to peak realization as human beings. Such faith was as total as could be imagined because most of the time we were not even conscious of what was happening inside us. Only when entering the so-called age of reason (which should really be called ages, because reasoning power is not attained in a scoop, but rather as a process) is that we begin to introspectively ask ourselves about the meaning of all our previous actions. This intellectual leap that characterizes our beginning of adolescence, and later adulthood, is characterized by the questioning of the faithful acceptance of what has been passed on by our ancestors. After a process of maturation, which can be varied in length, generally a fruitful marriage between faith and reason is established, by which the former is recognized, consciously or unconsciously, as the keystone. From such reasoned acceptance of previous ideas is that human beings can begin to construct their contribution to accumulated knowledge that will itself be passed onto future generations.

H) Acculturation through school and social interaction

From the role of the family in this process of transmitting knowledge, the contributions of schooling must be of underlined importance in the process, which is clearly underlined by their early appearance in the evolution of *homo sapiens sapiens*. This institution begins early in civilization in order to reinforce a process that begins in the familial background. Teachers begin to coach in our minds all that human beings have learned in a more deliberate and organized fashion beginning in *kindergarten*. All types of learning are passed on the premise of faith in our instructors, given that they are impossible of self-verification[17], especially when we are young. The importance of such transmission of knowledge is so large that it fills about one quarter of our lives, in contrast to the almost intuitive knowledge of the rest of the animal kingdom. A good part of our education consists of reinforcing in the child the confidence that it accomplishes intellectually and by willpower, which is clearly an expression of the faith mechanism. In addition to making the young aware of human potentialities, this reinforces the child's self-confidence and the latter is the essence of learning, without which we could not attain nor transmit knowledge, which requires that is confidently absorbed (nobody can give what they do not have).

The contributions of friendships, especially in childhood and adolescence, lies in the verification among children of the same age, that this knowledge has been received and transmitted. As we begin to approach, and eventually move to adulthood, learning becomes more conscious, and the exchange of experiences deepens, as we verify with friends at school neighborhood or social circles, that the right path has been followed. It is necessary to verify that what happens to us also occurs with others, and to know what we can be certain of to enjoy a well-balanced and socially integrated life. Adolescents are generally more open, sincere, and communicative than adults,

---

[17] Such faith consists in believing that our teachers know what they are transmitting.

because they are in greater need in the acquisition and transmission of knowledge and must mutually reinforce the auto credibility.

I) How Strong of a Force is Acculturation?

Even though recent research has raised the importance of genetic factors in determining behavior, particularly in their interaction with social and cultural factors, the importance of the latter is incredibly significant.

To be successful in life, every ethnic group, whether it is a nation or not, distills through the centuries of their existence a comport of useful experiences for a better living. The same process occurs at lower levels that subcategorize the group into geo-political subdivisions, ultimately reaching the level of the family. This temporal learning supplements the basic and subtle messages of faith and intuition of human beings, to which we have referred just above. The cultural and social conditioning that we now consider, aid in attaining life accomplishments that go beyond genetic conditioning. Acculturation changes how we think and act, in ways that improve the quality of human life. If these societal contributions to human growth and development are positive in balance, they can make possible a fuller existence.

This cultural knowledge is passed on from generation to generation and is the basis for the improvement of humanity. Such acculturation tends to strengthen our will, harden our motivation, and redoubles our efforts to apply one talent to the domination and development of the rich endowment that God has bestowed to us for our earthly life.

J) Customs, Habits, and Behavior

The social customs on which behavior is based eventually translate into institutions. Our communications with the Creator were eventually established when human beings in slow ascension fondly needed the stage of homo sapiens sapiens. As these customs extended throughout human societies, and their practices deepened, religious institutions were established. These bodies of social norms, concealed or not in institutions, become important determinants of human behavior. For example, a great part of our beliefs, and the actions from which they decant, are based on the social norm of purveying primary education to all our descendants, which began in the XVII century in Rome with Saint Joseph Calasanz, founder of the Piarists (Scolappi Dei).

But not only our activities and behavior are influenced by social customs, but also by individual habits that arise from them. Like customary behavior, habitual actions are ways to confront frequent situations in the gregarious life of human beings in the world; they constitute answers at the individual level of men, when confronted repeatedly with certain circumstances of daily living. Like customs, these habits determine human behavior patterns but are in themselves more perilous, given that these threaded reactions have not always been confronted with the results of social experience. This is clearly seen when our instinctive tendencies to protect ourselves from danger (the flight or fight syndrome) are exacerbated creating, among others, the habits of anxiety and timidity, which can have harmful consequences.

K) Do People Really Modify their Behavior?

The majority would respond negatively to this question. Habits and individual customs that have been acquired seem relentless. As the old Spanish adage tells us, we will be ourselves until death do us part ("genio y figura hasta la sepultura'). Many psychotherapists, perhaps most, also tend to think this way. You can show human beings how to manage, manipulate and adapt to their habits, but not to change them. If you are shy, this trait will accompany you for the rest of your life, yet you may learn how to control or vanquish it.

Yet, this way of focusing on habits does not consider the most important aspect of our personality, which is motivation and willpower. Decades ago, the famous Harvard psychologist B.F. Skinner

showed how behavior can be altered by exercising activism to inter-
cept the unexamined reactions that habits represent. It is also important to be aware of the automatic reactions involved in our routines.

But most importantly, it is enforcing the will, and having faith that
change can be achieved, as a motivating factor. Thus, habit attacks can
be controlled. This is just a lack of convincement that many times
boycotts the modification of our bad habits which deep down only
means that we are not ready to change our behavior patterns.

Yet, as the adage tells us, "The flesh is weak." What if the tendencies we would like to change are of the genetic or instinctive type,
rather than nurtured or epigenetic? Surely these are more difficult to
combat, but with willpower and faith, they can be destroyed in most
cases. In these circumstances the fundamental problem is the lack of
perseverance, because in this kind of processes change will come later
rather than sooner. A stronger willpower is needed under these circumstances, together with being fully hopeful that the planned modification of the undesirable behavior will surely come. It must be remembered that "faith can move mountains."

What cannot be changed most of the time, are the principal traits of
human personality. Some people are sanguineous, tending to be
extroverted, spontaneous and active. They are not concentrated in
themselves and prefer gregariousness and party-like behavior. Others
are cool and collected, introverted, calculating, passive and self-conscious, retired, and tranquil. To totally change a person is quite difficult. Even for these opposing personalities, it would be even cumber-
some to modify some of their traits, and make them more or less
inhibited, although partial modification may be more attainable than
a total change over. Notwithstanding the above, such modifications,
whether partial or total, have been accomplished with frequency,
particularly when faith and willpower accompany the efforts made.
Just recall the transformation the twelve apostles underwent from
simple fishermen to the founders of Christianity. From being extremely humble and insecure, to crusaders that exuded so much
self-confidence that they were capable of leading whole societies.
They were convinced that they were resembling images of God, and

as Saint Paul expressed and we have previously quoted, they thought that: "anything is within our powers by the grace of He who comforts me."

L) Summing Up: How Much Does One Know; How Much Does One Learn

More than half our potential with respect to knowing how to live our lives as fully and satisfactorily as possible, is already determined before our birth. We are genetically born with the conditions needed to successfully face the different phases of life, from infancy to old age, and to accumulate the knowledge and experience necessary to enjoy our existence and derive maximum welfare from it. Our personality and character and our most important traits, are primarily determined by our genetic endowment, congeniality and instinctively we are born with the abilities and capabilities which allow us to reason, express ourselves, move and emote, be self-conscious, communicate, etc. In addition, God has disposed from time immemorial when creating us in his image and resemblance, that we possess a soul or spirit implying an eternal life, and thus to calm the mysterious angst that lead to search for Him.

On the other hand, life renders us lessons practically since conception. The attributes and potentialities with which we are born, and the personalities and traits that characterize us, as fingerprints, develop because of our relationships with others. Genetics may incline towards certain behavioral patterns, but it is not entirely deterministic of our behavior. The potential implicit in our genetic endowment is fully realized through the process of social learning. The accumulation of knowledge implicit in social relations also tends to generate habits and customs that shape human personalities and behavior, even though these are more malleable to the forces that willpower and faith can attain.

Natural and acquired traits are as well the origin of personality problems and common neurotic inclinations common to men, as well as their mental infirmities. Again, most of them are due to genetic or natural forces, and less to the epigenetic factors of acculturation and nurturing, which can be controlled with greater ease.

However, the greater part of mental and behavioral deficiencies consists in the repetition of erroneous behavior patterns as pointed out by psychologist Wayne Dyer in his book *Your Erroneous Zones*. By exercising human willpower, supported by a solid base of faith, this repetitiveness can be confronted. Success is accomplished by changing certain patterns of behaving, emoting, and acting, for more healthy ones, until the latter become repetitive, thus displacing the previous unhealthy ones. It is important to underline that the first life of unhealthy and mistaken-laden behavior patterns should never be fought against, but rather they should be replaced by more positive and healthier ones. In the end, it is customs and habits, be they for good or bad, that determine our being. And since freewill is the principal moving force, it is within our realm to prefer those that improve our actions and personality.

IV

THROUGHT, EMOTION, IMAGINATION AND BEHAVIOR

A) A Straight-Line Relation or Interaction

Human behavior, as has brrn explained in the previous chapter, is determined by genetic or innate tendencies (mostly) and by social conditioning or epigenetic forces (the least). These are the strongest determinants in general terms.

When the forces that define how human beings act are examined in greater detail, a conjunction of them that derive from these two must be considered. These are the thinking and emoting processes of men and women, as well as their imagination. Those constitute the immediate tendencies that determine their actions, but it must be accepted that occasionally these relations are inverted, with the latter influencing the former. But generally, as we think, we imagine; and as we imagine, we emote. And as we emote, we behave.

Rational-emotive or cognitive behavior psychologists are those that have analyzed with greater success and dedication how thoughts, imagination and emotions have influenced human behavior. Given one of the continuous stimuli experienced by human beings, a chain of thoughts appears, which can be rational (positive or optimistic) or irrational (negative or pessimistic). When the latter prevails, they are followed by irrational and negative images, which end up conveying negative and irrational behavior. Therefore, the beginning of this chain of irrational and negative activities, are the same type of thoughts. Only by changing these thoughts can neurotic behavior be overcome (the latter being defined by stupid behavior of intelligent human beings). These thoughts represent the internalization of our own thoughts, through which we talk to ourselves, and they take place continually in our minds even though most of the time we are not consciously aware of them.

The first to write about these concepts was Dr. Albert Ellis who stated his rational-emotive theory of human behavior in the 1950s. He was one of the leading exponents of modern psychotherapy, which has attempted to improve the outcomes of many persons that suffer problems of neurosis, phobias, anxiety, and obsessive-compulsive behavior, confronting their apparently immediate causes, in contrast with the psychoanalytic approach. These novel techniques have emphasized the focusing on cognition, rationalizations, and the apparent beliefs that are expressed through the thinking process, and which determine our emotional reactions and our behavior.

B) What is Thought?

Even though thought tends to be the independent variable in the group of mental experiences that have been described above, it must be recognized that in this process there is much important feedback. Many times, our actions and emotions end up influencing our thoughts. When in an *impromptu* fashion a meeting takes place in the office, which we cannot avoid, if we tend to be a timid person, a series of irrational thoughts will come into our mind, that will bring forth negative emotions, that will make us to act nervously and to experience sensations brought about by the "flight or fight" syndrome mentioned in a previous chapter. However, if we overcome these emotions and subsequent behavior by generating new calm thoughts and emotions, or by forcing, through willpower and faith, our organism to speak, smile, relax, etc., it won't be long before these new emotions and behavior come to generate positive thoughts, thus changing the sign of the original independent variable, now turned into a dependent variable. If we modify our behavior in this fashion on repeated occasions for a given amount of time, we will end up changing these quite common tendencies toward timidity which affect 40 percent of human beings.

Thus, it is explained how the electro-chemical impulses that constitute our thoughts influence the other psychological activities of the human body, which are also based in these types of impulses. Equally, it can be shown how in our organism these are interactive exchanges through which the electro-chemical reactions that undergird our emoting and behaving, do influence our thoughts.

From a psycho-linguistic and philosophic approach, thoughts are groups of ideas and concepts without beginning or end. We are always stringing these thoughts in a continuous fashion. Every record of our day is filled with thinking, and in a tenth of a second, various thoughts are stringed together. Generally, we are not conscious of our thoughts, but if an effort is made, we can discover what they are. In this sense it is not correct to consider that we are moved by our unconscious or our subconscious. What should be recognized that happen and be aware of the danger is that this string of thoughts and concepts, potentially conscious, can deepen the impact of the negative and irrational thoughts over our emotions and behavior. In such repetition of irrational thoughts, there is the danger that they may become increasingly more catastrophic and disastrous, thus multiplying the negative intensity of the emotions and behavior. The process tends even more towards panic and hysteria, when the feedback of the subsequent emotional and behavioral reactions, leads to even more negative or irrational thinking. This process takes place through the words and sentences that we address ourselves, and which in essence constitute conversations we have with ourselves, or that we internalize in our interior.

C) What is emotion?

Up to now it has been shown that thoughts are the dominant factor in our behavior. But in certain cases, we first have to emote before acting. In these situations, there is an intermediate process between thinking and acting, which is influenced by the former. That intervening step is emoting. What does this emotion consist of? In our opinion, it is nothing more than a biased thought. This is why it is not surprising that when in the previous paragraph we considered the retro feeding of emotions over thoughts, it was established that this happened through conversations we had addressing ourselves, generally in internal fashion (but sometimes by speaking out loud to ourselves).

Emotions are in their essence thoughts, which are so permeated with sentiments and imagery, that it is difficult to perceive how much prejudiced thinking they consist of. Therefore, when the emotional is articulated through a feedback process, they become prejudiced thought, laying here how they reflect biased emotions. The irrationality laid bare in this process affects our mound thinking, transforming it into irrational thoughts. However, it should be understood that some of these emotions are negative, while others are positive, because some sentiments produce images of love and goodness, while others bring forth those of fright and hate.

Finally, emotions are thoughts laden with value judgments, and generally self-evaluative of the person and their actions. Some of these evaluations are favorable and others unfavorable, but generally they are not well balanced. "We are not as remarkable as sometimes it is our belief, or as limited as other times we think," according to the Jesuit psychologist and Biblicist Juan Cortés, Ph.D. When we frequently judge our actions, they raise as much to our awareness that it becomes difficult to behave intuitively, which is what leads to our best performance. Even though emotions derive from thoughts, it must not be forgotten that when the former are negative, they are potentially destructive. Particularly when we recognize how they can retro feed our thought processes. This is why it is important to control our emotions.

D) What is a Prejudiced or Biased Thought?

It is a non-objective thought which judges and evaluates. Not from a moral, ethical, or religious standpoint, but with respect to a level of subjective comparison which is self-defined. To begin with, human beings tend to establish extremely high reference points. No wonder, as Alfred Adler used to say, we feel inferior. These emotive thoughts, therefore, conspire against the objective of attaining rationality, because they are laden with a chain of irrational thoughts, which tend to be negative and obsessive. That is why this sequence must be interrupted, and we must strive to do the best we can; without judging our performance, or evaluating our actions, because the latter introduces the element of doubt in our behavior.

Emotion is as well a prejudiced or biased thought which tends to follow a particular tendency, proclivity, or path, changing a given stimulus to a corresponding emotional reaction. After a while this becomes an unthought or irrational habit or custom which leads us, for example, to feel inhibition, and then fright when we come close to the border of a ledge in a tall building.

Finally, it is thinking that presupposes something, usually without any basis for it. Thus, when a particular situation is faced, *ipso facto* a biased thought appears (that is an emotion) which colors our reaction to the original stimulus. For example, if a person has reverential fright towards another, and this individual suddenly appears, a biased thought (or emotion) of inferiority complex emerges and the subject is laden by anxiety and tension, and the reaction that comes to the fore during the exchange between them, will be colored by the frightful and inferiority feelings of the person influenced by the emotions and biases. All these patterns result from the unfounded assumption that the person being interacted with is superior to us.

E) What is the Role of Imagining?

As a reaction to a perception from the senses, images are generated. When an appetizing food is seen (the stimulus), the pleasure that we would feel while eating it, is imagined (the reaction) and we salivate (the action).

Not always do the stimuli provoke a set of so well-defined consequences as in the example above. On many occasions the reaction is a thought, other times it is an emotion (an irrational thought) and infrequently an image. Yet in many circumstances we find the images mixed with the thoughts and emotions, or the thoughts and emotions intertwined.

It is quite common that the images or stimuli do precipitate irrational thoughts, and emotions, in a chain reaction, as the mind is frequently prone to make possible. For example, when at a certain age certain things are forgotten for a short span of time, an image or reaction might come to us, in which we see ourselves in a nursing home without recognizing anyone. This is succeeded by a negative thought that concludes that we are already suffering from Alzheimer's disease, and as a result we might decide not to partially refrain from certain social activities, like playing cards.

Generally, the images that are produced are well defined, even in an exaggerated fashion. They tend to be positive or pleasing or quite negative and hurtful. The descriptions above represent good examples of the mental processes in question.

F) To What Extent all of the Above Influences Behavior?

As we behave in accordance with our thoughts, emotions, and images, that are negative or irrational, our behavior will be prejudiced. It follows that such biased behavior will reinforce our thoughts, emotions and imagery through the feed-process described earlier. But, although willpower and having faith in modifying behavior, a change in our reactions is obtained, this process will accomplish a modification of our images, emotions, and biased and irrational thoughts. In actuality, mind and body have compensatory mechanisms that are automatic, which stop these chains of unidirectional actions and reactions, whether they are positive or negative. Suddenly, contrarian thoughts, sentiments or images emerge, and our behavior begins to change accordingly, until the pendulum swings in the opposite direction.

Furthermore, on many occasions the best therapy is that involving actions and behavior. This is based on the knowledge that if we act in a certain way, going against our psychological weaknesses, we are first of all involving willpower and faith, in an affirmative act of free will. Immediately, thoughts, emotions and images of a positive merit are counterposed to the irrational and biased thoughts, and negative sentiments and imagery. And change is initiated. Immediately afterwards, the behavioral change has a visceral effect which, through the interactions between body and mind, reinforces the positive messages that are expressed through the previous voluntary steps mentioned just above. This scheme has been found to be extraordinarily successful in combatting phobias and irrational fears.[18]

Placing ourselves in these situations by choice, and exercising the force of willpower and faith, will generate the positive thoughts that allow us to understand that these are just imaginary worries and dangers, which are devoid of reality. When these rational thoughts are set in opposition to the irrational ones suggesting that something terrible is about to happen, if we experience the stimulus that frightens us, the newly minted rational thought that emerges from our actions, is followed by positive images and emotions that reinforce it. When these actions are frequently repeated, senseless fears dissipate, and the habits that had fostered them begin to crumble, and we recover our good sense in the evaluation of the situations, in an incremental fashion.

G) Rational and Irrational Thoughts

The thoughts and emotions (biased thinking) that come to our mind are of these two types. What defines if thoughts are rational? Ultimately if they help human beings to attain their temporal and transcendental objectives. In contrast, irrationality conspires against human goals. As human evolution is a recent phenomenon, in the *homo sapiens, sapiens phase*, we still have irrational tendencies as an atavic trait. In fact, neurosis is another name for irrationality, which can be defined as an intelligent being thinking and acting stupidly. On the other hand, when we give a lot of thoughts to a matter, or accept what others have concluded about it, we reach conclusions to which a deal

---

[18]   In English the term fear has been used by psychologists of a clinical bent to stand for F (false), E(evidence), A (appearing), R (real). Which translates to like False Evidence Appearing as Real.

of trust is given. These are what we have called beliefs. They result from the powers of our rational thinking, and in them the peak of rationality is accomplished. When they are expressed as thoughts, and attain consciousness, they can be distinguished from others because of their permanency.

Although these thoughts-beliefs are basically immutable because they are firmly based on faith, belonging to the essence of our being, the other ephemeral thoughts, whether rational or irrational (some of which, because they are biased or prejudiced can result in emotions), have their *raison d'etre*. They warn us of dangers, whether real or imagined. Given that their function is quite different, they do not constitute part of our essence. Thus, they can never be allowed to question it. A human being is increasingly balanced if it learns to distinguish between these two types of thoughts, to take advantage of their differences, and to learn how not to be affected (or to loath) the irrational ones, by recognizing how they can be useful as warning signals.[19]

H) How do Beliefs Accumulate?

Beliefs arise not only from knowledge distilled from deep and continuous thoughts about a subject matter, from which conclusions are derived. Some are implicit to the essence of our humanness, and are intuitive. These are the things known to us at the time of birth, as the exercise of our will, which is automatically put to work to learn about the principles of life without any self-examination, up to the time when reasoning begins to be used. This body of knowledge is basic and accompanies us as intrinsic knowledge from the time of our birth, constituting part of the essence, nucleus, or center of every human being, and it is positive or good given that we are created in God's image and likeness.

Some beliefs are also forged from the inductive process implicit in those experiences that result from living, and from the accumulated

---

[19] As has been pointed out, their origin can be traced to our atavist flght or fight syndrome.

experience of life. As has been written above, in one of the meetings of Greek philosophers at the agora, a sophist indulged in dispositions about the simplest traits of human behavior, which at the same time constitute the representation of its essence.[20] Diogenes, one of the most distinguished members of the contending school of cynics asked him: "What are you thinking about? The reply was: "How is it that we can walk?" To which with cynicism Diogenes stood up and started walking, while responding "This is how we do it." These experiences result in cumulative beliefs that are inserted in our positive essence and allow us to act and express ourselves as human beings in our earthly existence.

It should be noted that in putting together our beliefs and truths, which begin inside our mother's womb, there is a high content of rationality, as defined through our deductions and inductions. In the same way, the support that faith offers to this core or nucleus of affirmed beliefs is fundamental. But there is also an important content of positivism or practicality, which leads us to believe in those things that work, or that help us to attain our goals and aspirations. While certain methods or objectives become a reality, and shown to work in practice, and resolve our problems, we continue to believe in them. We believe that tylenol, for example, will get rid of our headache, without being able to explain how it happens. Until it is invalid, that belief will be one of many in the essence of our being. Considering the alternatives of asking ourselves if it is really the medicine, or the placebo effect what takes care of our headache, or trusting the medicine without further questioning, it is clearly more convenient to do the latter, and make it part of the cumulative beliefs in the essence of our being. If this works and solves our problems, it is what we will do.

---

[20] Sophism constituted a philosophical school that dwelled in such discourse given their belief that man was the measure of all things, and the debate about movement between Heraclitus and Parmenides.

I) Are Emotions Negative or Positive?

Neither one nor the other. This should be assessed according to the results. Even though this may seem surprising, many things in life are defined arbitrarily, and through faith. And even though it may appear out of place and irrational, this is due to the constraints which limit our limited human mind. Is the mind simply supposing in these cases that in order to have beliefs, which in themselves have a high content of faith, it is necessary to have a feeling of belief, together with a thought that convinces us that the matter is believable?

It must be realized that one of the most powerful mechanisms of our knowledge, which is mathematically expressed logic, has developed by basing itself in arbitrary and counterintuitive assumptions, and even then, has ended up describing unsuspected real phenomena.[21] This is why it must be understood that a good number of negative emotions help us survive, as the panic that makes us run when a bull is coming our way. While positive emotions can lead us to death, as when we feel an attraction to a woman known as having frequent affairs, and thus a good candidate for a sexual disease, and we still go to bed with her.

It must be acknowledged, however, that emotions, being in themselves biased thoughts, must be dealt with differently in our behavior, requiring the assistance of faith and willpower. Emotions are more easily recognized than thoughts because they awaken our conscience in a more vivid way; yet they are more difficult to control than the latter. Yet, we must underline that what is important are not our thoughts and emotions, but rather what we do and how we behave, and this is fundamentally determined by our beliefs,[22] (which are our deepest thoughts, and happen to be those that are more rational and pristine), our faith, and our believing willpower.

---

[21] Some postulates of mathematical logic cannot be proven to be true or false.

[22] Or as Jesus said, "by the abundance of your heart."

J) The Real Measure of Our Rationality is Our Behavior

As is evident from what has been discussed above, many forces act upon us internally, some rational and others irrational, some positive and others negative. They are expressed through beliefs, emotions, thoughts, and images. Some of them are consciously perceived while others are not, at a given moment. These are ultimately molded to a higher or lower degree by our faith and willpower, which are determined by the liberty to act that God has given us. These beliefs, emotions, thoughts, and images are continuously changing, constituting a set of variable forces. From all this it is our actions that result, which are also susceptible to change, but that constitute the real essence of our being, and the real measure of our rationality. This is the kernel in the evangelical phrase "by his achievements (or fruits) you will know who they are." The gathering of contradictory forces that precede our actions are frequently not perceived by our conscience, and to a great degree constitute needed considerations to ensure that we are acting adequately. They reflect the worries of human beings about their behavior, and it is normally to be expected, even though in certain cases it can become repetitive questioning. It is quite common that this group of thoughts and emotions that precede behavior, could be discovered through the examination of the facial or bodily expressions of the persons.

In order to place the above in an appropriate content, it must be recognized that the thoughts, emotions, images, and feelings only exist in our minds. They are not part of real life to take place outside our wind minf, and on many occasions, they constitute fantasies while in others they are internalized mental games or internal debates. However, these unreal or imaginary considerations are like temptations, which are not sins unless we allow ourselves to be influenced by them. But what is determinant in sinning, as in our all other more frequent actions, is the power of our will, based on our beliefs.

K) The essence of Our Beliefs Controls our Behavior.

After what may be heavy mental and emotional comings and goings, human beings are guided by their group of beliefs, which lay in the essence of our minds. This process is accomplished automatically, not needing our conscious involvement, even though we can consciously become aware of it if so desired. Operatively, however, the set of beliefs that informs, and is informed by our faith, utilizes our willpower to accomplish the actions and stances that constitute our behavior.

Thus, the essence of our beliefs remains impervious in the face of the multitude of thoughts, emotions, images, sentiments, prejudices, etc., that quickly interpose one to another successfully every minute of our life. Such essence constitutes the base, center, or nucleus of our being, and resides in our spirit. This essential core of our being is the force that allows us to control our nervousness, fights, pressures, anxieties, anguish, and mental paralysis that confront us daily, and end up performing to accomplish our chores, responsibilities, and goals.

It is in our spirit where the essence of our beliefs resides, but also where our faith and goodness find their abode. We have all been created in the image and likeness of God. Our soul is equivalent to what we have been calling our essence or spirit. In the same manner our willpower is equally and fundamentally expressed in the initiatives that arise from this essential basis of our being. It must be recognized, however, that this spiritual center of our humanity also harbors a negative component which we must always be on guard against. From this dark side originate doubts about us, temptations, unlawful thoughts, etc., which originate from the negative part of our essence. We should never pay attention to these expressions of original sin in our being, because in doing so we will only facilitate the growth of such negativity in the nucleus of our spirit, which would offer it the opportunity to expand its influence over our behavior. This is why it is so important to develop our instincts and intuition, so that they would allow us to distinguish and pursue the incitement of our minds to distinguish what belongs to the positive part of our essence, from those that arise from its negative component.

V

FREE WILL, WILLPOWER AND FAITH

A) Predestination and Freedom

Some believe, and a portion of them are sophisticated, that our destiny in life is predetermined. Curiously many of these persons are atheists, but in the end, they have to recognize that they believe in a superhuman authority, that even if they would not want to deify, is even more powerful than the Creator, because it determines their thoughts, feelings, emotions and actions, because how could it otherwise control destiny. Of course, if a person chooses to accept such ideas, it will live as arbitrarily as such belief represents, because human rationality has provided sufficient support to faith, to understand that our essential quality is freedom, and that God allows us to forge our own destiny.

B) Destiny and Change: Challenges to Free Will

Returning to the idea of predestation and the force of destiny, in the previous section it has been stated that it lacks substantial basis, whether by applying reason or faith. However, an additional challenge that has arisen, even if partially, is that human beings have a limited number of alternatives or options. Thus, freewill is constricted to this constrained set of alternatives. Certainly, this is true, but it must be understood that the concept of freewill abhors the idea of decrepitude, which goes against the dignity of men. In trying to amplify our choices goes even further, and can attain the extreme behavior of original sin, which consisted in wanting to have the power of electing among all possible things.

As a creature, a human being could never be compared with God, because she exists independently from Him, even though created in his image. Being part of creation, it is applicable to him the famous phrase of the Archangel Saint Michael Quis ut Deus? ("Who can be like God"). Man's freedom is limited, which can, although it should not, end in licentiousness. However, the limits of this freedom are quite wide, and this allows him to taste the essence of divine liberty. The concept of human nature is the determining factor of these parameters, which are sufficiently wide to allow her to experience the quality, received as a gift, of free will. Yet, the key attribute that characterizes our humanity is that, even though the range of the possibilities of choice is quite wide, it is from the beginning limited by the limits of our worldly existence.

C) How Much Can People Change?

Those that brought forth the school of conditioned behavior at Harvard, following the leadership of Professor Skinner, consider that the animal kingdom, including *homo sapiens sapiens* follow daily life of habit and routine. Once we establish a way of doing things, we tend to respect it. And our lives become an accumulation of repetitions. However, there is an escape hatch! In the same way habits that condition us are created, other habits can be established that decondition us from those that have been established. That habitual behavior is not like time, that up to now we can only know how to accompany it by marching in the same direction: it can go backwards. Any person that behaves habitually can break the habit. To think that we must live personally chained to our habits is a fallacy, because any path that is followed can be walked back. My uncle Justo Carrillo, an unforgettable character with whom many paths were shared, used to tell me: "a human being should not be the slave of anything, not even of the idea of not being a slave of anything." Clearly, to overcome bad habits (the good ones should be kept) again we have relied on faith and willpower, and in addition to hardly press towards change.

In order to substitute new routines for those that bedevil us an that we want to replace, it is essential to control our emotions. Many believe that this is practically impossible or extremely hard. This is because we are confused about what an emotion consists of. Understanding, as has been explained before, consists of a prejudiced thought, then it is understood that what we think can really be changed. Our thoughts are part of our load of central beliefs, which are in a moment, and that are based on our faith. It should be stressed that it is tied to freewill, without which we would be like the rest of the animal kingdom, ruled only by our instincts. If this were not the case, we could elect not to sin. Thus, by understanding that emotions are based on the thoughts that originated them, it is easier for us to accept that they can be changed, and thus to modify our habits. This is so because the permanence of the latter is tied to the emotive shock needed to break away from these types of behavior. There are so many strong emotions created by these thoughts (many times initially subconscious) that are biased or implicit emotions in deviating from the old routines, or the establishment of new ones, that we end up accepting the impossibility of these attempts. And do not grasp that we have to proceed by ignoring these emotions, and changing them as we do with thoughts, which in the end is what they essentially are, and in their essence prejudiced ones.

D) *Possunt Quia Posse Videntur*

This aphorism is attributed to the philosopher Tertulian. This concept later on influenced the ideas of Saint Augustine. The latter makes clear the power of faith (to which everything is attainable), in the sense that if we can see, feel, and conceive ourselves as being able to do something, and capable of performing it, we would surely be able to undertake it. This idea follows in the same vein as Saint Paul's statement: "I can do anything in He who comforts me," which has been previously mentioned. The belief that we can accomplish it is the premise for any of our undertakings. The principle is the following, which derives from the Latin meaning: "they can because they see themselves doing it."

What is pointed out here is the basis of a technique that has been developed in the last few decades in the psychology of athletics. It invokes the athlete to imagine that he is accomplishing the feats that he is accomplishing, the feats that he is attempting to perform. The repetition of these images, just before attempting the desired athletic result, reinforces the faith and confidence that his desired accomplishment can be attained. Repeating these images is very important for the attainment of athletic objectives. This technique can also be applied to similar objectives in other endeavors, and generally. Moreover, when we practice for any performance, we are following a procedure like the imagining just described, because there is a close relationship between performance and training. Although it is not common to identify it in such a fashion, it seems clear that perhaps the most productive part of these repetitions is the confidence it generates that we can accomplish what we will be attempting to do.

Certainly, the power of self-confidence, or faith in ourselves, as we have most frequently called it in this monograph, is crucial to accomplishing any endeavor. Although we may have doubts in the undertaking of anything (and as we have previously said, these can be convenient, as they make us aware of negative thoughts) if we have faith in ourselves at the level of our deepest beliefs, we will be successful in our accomplishments. Furthermore, it is possible to extend this, and affirm that, if we first have faith on our side, everything will be attained as an extension of it. To end this section with a well-known proverb: "if we have faith, we shall move mountains."

E) Faith, Self-Confidence, and Convincement

To have self-confidence, it is necessary to have faith, and to have faith, self-confidence is required.[23] Even though this appears to be an

---

[23] Both are ultimately graces or divine gifts, even though they can be consciously developed.

enigmatic statement, it is only another application of a basic principle of psychology and spirituality: if we do not have it, we cannot give it. Symbiosis is produced because of quasi-simultaneous interaction among the main forces of humankind, which impedes the determination of which comes first. A similar concept was discussed earlier, when determining which comes first: faith or knowledge (*Fides querens intellectum* or vice versa). In this other chicken or egg case, it seems to us that faith is the precedent because it is the basis and gives rise to self-confidence and self-worth.

But from then on, the latter two can be defined as faith in oneself, and which can be extended to all human activity, because in doing so we would only be giving what we already have.

Confidence or faith in oneself allows a realistic self-examination. If this were not the case, the vision we would have of ourselves would necessarily be biased, and thus would be a wrong one. And this does not necessarily mean that we would see ourselves inferior to others, as we could also, although not as frequently, have an exaggerated view of ourselves. Although as has been said previously, the normal tendencies of human beings are those that make them feel inferior. But remember, what one feels is not necessarily what one believes.

This same maxim applies to the possibility of being oneself. Only with self-confidence can we behave as we really are. If not, we would be continuously trying to cover our weaknesses and defects, rather than accepting them in front of others, and ourselves. Only by recognizing and accepting with total trust what we are, can we change and improve. We must be genuine with ourselves interlay, and accept what we are, and behave according to our real personality and characteristics. Self-doubts, like self-aggrandizement, come from lack of confidence and faith in ourselves, which lead us away from behaving as we really are, and change to what we could become.

F) The Interactions between Faith and Willpower

The crux of all existence is that our individuality is as valuable, no less and no more, as that of any other human being. Any panther, pig, lamb, or goat is like others of the same species. Distinctions are introduced by humans; my dog or cat is better than those of my neighbor. This can be extended to the inanimate world: my house or car is better than my neighbor's (and of course my enemy). But there is an implicit trap in this reasoning because we tend to believe that if we grant the opposite, there is an implicit reflection on ourselves, and we then feel inferior. This non-sequitur is as common as not believing that all human beings are equal.

But we are not convinced at all in the value of faith and self-confidence. Human beings can change themselves if they genuinely accept their own self-worth, while recognizing that unless they have trust that they can do it will not be possible. And it is difficult to achieve such convincement without faith in a superior being, that would have imprinted on us the spirituality that is necessary to conquer the fickle matter of our bodies. This is why, throughout history, the most developed and thus successful peoples have had profound religious beliefs. The matter of which we are made is evidently a decaying one and is a vessel that serves to either condemn or redeem us. The determining factors are the spiritual qualities already mentioned: faith, confidence, and willpower; the paradigms of our spiritual mind or soul.

G) Acceptance, Uncertainty and Change

There is something extremely important, and curious at the same time in the process of change. It is that unless we accept ourselves, it will be impossible to change. The acceptance of what you are is the "open sesame" to the stream of new behavior that makes us change. Magically, as soon as the barrier of not or partial acceptance of ourselves is breached, our behavior is modified with fluidity and easiness.

Self-acceptance is a form of self-esteem, self-love and it is well known how love changes things. God created the Universe out of love, and sustains us through it, given that it is the only cosmological force. Therefore, unless we ourselves love, even the band and the ugly in this world, we will not be able to change it because love is the power that changes everything (amor vincit omnia). As we should not loose sleep about future or uncertain events, which after all cannot be predicted, and again lovingly accept them, and thus derive from them the greatest joy, in the understanding that they flow from the divine will, the designs of which we cannot now understand.

If we want to change our defects, weaknesses, imperfections, addictions, psychological problems, and other similar circumstances, we must introduce and add a good new behavior, instead of trying to eliminate and erase the bad old ones. This begins with the acceptance of the latter, as we have just written, but we have to go further. Once we understand the reason and functioning that originate and sustain our negative tendencies, we should not worry about frontally fighting them, because when we do, they will strengthen as we underline their importance and give undeserved attention. In turn, we should substitute positive tendencies in their place, concentrating our willpower in the latter, ensuring that they will be strengthened by the attention we pay them, and by thus forming new habits.

H) Self-Confidence and Knowledge

Our basic beliefs, the basis of our essence, are deep and stable. This is why, when we are convinced of something, it is not normal that it will be continuously brought to our mind. This nucleus of basic and effective knowledge is what fundamentally orients our behavior. Our diverse types of weaknesses generally result from reactions to a series of biased thoughts that only populate the superficiality of our being, but because of habits or confusion, they momentarily subjugate us. But soon after the profundity of our beliefs overcome them, our behavior is changed accordingly.

In contrast with the subjacent stability of our basic thoughts, the thoughts and emotions that visit our mind, are fundamentally unstable. Many of them are expressions of a point-counterpoint fashion, being fundamentally diverse, mostly being like light streams disappearing from our conscience to return in uncertain periods. They only remain when bolstered by normative thoughts, our emotions that request our attention (such as habits, worry, doubt and certain or imagined dangers), or because being bothersome, it pushes us to notice them wanting their banishment.

Our central and innate beliefs predominate when they collide with opposing contradictory thoughts, determining in the end our actions, which represent the legitimate part of our living. These constitute the real essence of our beliefs, defined by our faith, and defended by our will. Because we have firm confidence in them, they are given the power to regulate our behavior. And this is why, if our beliefs are mistaken, their modification is the basis for curing our erroneous tendencies. Faith in yourself is essential for allowing your deep-down beliefs to guide your life.

I) The Role of Doubt

Many people agonize, suffer and doubt about doubts. Yet they fail to understand that they are not bad in themselves. Without them, we would not discover the truth. Rene Descartes, the famous French philosopher physicist, and mathematician uttered another famous phrase: "Doubt is the origin of wisdom." How else would it be possible to discover the truth? In what fashion would it be possible to amplify the essence of our beliefs further than the instinctive and intuitive ways that God implants in our minds? In addition, doubts help us to guard ourselves from uncertain and dangerous situations. If bad doubts would not flood our mind at bay moments, in how many mistaken ways we would have travelled, and in how many disasters we would have participated? Do not fear doubts, rather welcome them.

Many are confused by the fallacy that doubts open parentheses in our lives that will cost much in time and effort to close. But this is not the case, because we can allot a reasonable amount of time to harbor them, and then take a decision about them. In many cases this would be instantaneously. Furthermore, doubting does not in any way compromise our faith, self-confidence, and beliefs. The substantial majority of the doubts we have about the latter are only preventive thoughts that help us reaffirm them.

For our beliefs to be rock-solid, they need to have gone through the challenge of doubt, which denudes them of their self-evidence, or clean them through reason and faith, allowing us to perceive what they really are. Doubt and humanity are one and the same, as we have just explained, as "dubitatio" like "errare," "humanum est." But it is essential to distinguish between doubts to discover the truth, and those that allow us to be preventive. The latter are only thoughts that put us on guard, like the common "flight or fight syndrome." They are useful, as they make us aware of our biased thoughts (emotions), that conflict with our faith and beliefs, and that end up reaffirming them.

VI

MENS SANA IN CORPORE SANO

A) Mind, Body and Spirit: The Interaction

If there is something we can be sure of, it is the interaction of these three concepts. Although this does not mean that there is not an order of importance in the same, as the latter dominates. The other two are intrinsically intertwined. Yet, in some sense, the mind is part of the body, but in another it is not. Through the spirit we influence mind and body, within the limitations given by natural laws. However, specially gifted people can govern these limitations occasionally. Mind and body can influence each other, although it is more common for the former to influence the latter.

The spirit or the soul are the alpha and the omega of this interaction. Why is this so? Because our spirituality, which is our essence, resides there. In the electric sparks and chemical reactions of the mind or brain, we will never find the spiritual compass. We are still conducting experiments in order to explain how thoughts, sentiments, emotions, beliefs, etc., are produced from the inanimate elements that compose our gray matter, and science is still far from understanding it as an endogenous process. It is difficult to believe that at what point we will be able to know how we arrived, without divine influence, to explain how matter can produce animic results. Even less now in the post-modernism state, in which positivism and reason are no longer trusted.

The direction of our life can be found in our spirit, which is the center and essence of our being. There is where our conscience resides, through which we not only perceive ethically, but are also able to judge, and where our pondering about good and evil implicitly resides, which makes humans moral beings. And ethical principles not established by human beings themselves but referred to the eternal and supreme being that created us, and who is essentially different to what he created. This is why we direct our body and soul to believe in accordance with the principles of conduct dictated by our religiosity.

B) Psychosomatic Manifestations

The ego is the self-centered part of our interior being. It cares about itself first of all. It is where our consciousness of ourselves as a different being is expressed. It is where our self-worth resides as well as our self-trust. All this determines that the marks that our self-worry leave in our mind are well delineated. When this psychological trait predominates, our brain is predisposed to certain reactions reflecting, for example, the habit of trying to attain personal satisfaction and to avoid frustration.

The super-ego exercises vigilance over the ego, placing limits on its reactions. It is the conscience of what is good or evil, based on our moral principles, in turn depending fundamentally on our religiosity and the values received from family, school and society. When through our psyche we convince ourselves that our actions are wrong, our conscience lead our brain (mind) to emit certain substance generally known as enkefalins, and the whole organism reacts with a sentiment of culpability that pervades all of the inner linings of our being, even though we could not become totally aware of it. Just the opposite occurs when we behave in accordance with our moral principles.

The two tendencies in question were described by Sigmund Freud as the principal movers of human behavior. They are expressed through our mind and reverberate in psychosomatic reactions that start with chemical substances and electric pulsations exchanged in our brains. These two main forces are enhanced by a third one; the id, which represent the tempestuous of our animal desires, from libido to avarice and the other capital sins which oppose the cardinal and theological virtues. Freud gave a vital importance to this latter force in molding, from childhood, the fundamental characteristic that shaped our psychic. In our opinion, especially in sexual tendencies, the proponent of psychoanalysis erred, because the ego and the super-ego are more relevant and important in explaining human behavior.

C) More Strictly Physiological Problems

The erroneous thoughts and emotions subjacent in the unconscious or subconscious of our psychic, can be conducive to corporal sickness. It is frequent that through a sense of culpability, or a repressed inferiority feeling, their escape valves may generate asthma or allergies. In these cases, the primary source of the problem must be considered for curation, and not the palliation of the secondary effects. This would require bringing to the surface and unmasking the untruthful premises subjacent in the mind, which, according to which has been shown in Chapter V, is entirely possible.

In the post-modern world it is frequent to suffer from anguish and anxiety. They result from the pressures of life resulting from work, family, and society. In some cases, we are not aware of these problems, while in others, most frequently, we do not know how to solve them, or we resist tackling in an appropriate fashion. It is easier to develop chronic head or back aches and attack them with medicines. After all, these symptoms are real, and this way out is easier than confronting the fact that their origin is psychological. The latter would imply recognizing an apparent personality deficiency and confronting the stigma withdrawal as such problems are still perceived (although increasingly more understandably) in society. And in addition, slower and prologued psychological and or psychiatric treatment. The easiest path leads us to deviate our focus from the true problem and push forth.

A similar comment could be applied to the somatic reactions that depression produces. Moreover, it is very frequent to experience a very close interaction between depressive and anxiety phenomena because, as it appears that we cannot get rid of one, it is easily intermingled with the other. Which of course strengthens the physiological manifestations of psychological ills.

D) More Strictly Psychological Problems

It is also common to encounter mental manifestations of neurosis. Like the corporal infirmities we have just addressed, which impede attaining the maxim which is the title of this chapter equally well a series of weaknesses in our psychic bring about this outcome, as they place obstacles in our reasoning. Thus, to accomplish a straight path reasoning, they must be confronted. The most common are those behavior patterns implicit in neurosis, (a term which is not as commonly used, and has not been adequately replaced) a common suffering of human beings.

Other psychological ills beckon from the disharmony in human behavior that come about from the frequent obsessive and/or compulsive syndromes that afflict humankind. These ills in our psyche that come about from these deviations from rationality are different from the unreasonable behavior brought about from neurosis, as they consist of habitual repetition of certain irrational reactions. Thus, the rainbow of our possible actions is constricted by the pre-selections that the obsessive-compulsive mechanism automatically undertakes for us.

Our mental sanity is finally challenged by other basic mental infirmities that afflict the modern man, which in their variety, make them submit to one or the other. These are emotional fears, insecurities, and anxiety. Even the first one noted could be considered part of the symptoms obsessive-compulsive behaviors, and the latter is a facet of neurosis, the commonality of these syndromes suggest that they should be given separate consideration. Agoraphobia is described as fright of situations in which either space, or contact with the public, produce impressions that make us behave as if dominated by an irrational fear. The lack of self-esteem is quite a generalized psychological problem, as the insecurity it brings about impedes our decisions based on well-pondered thoughts and opinions.

E) The Treatment of These Problems

First, we must recognize that the causative thought processes in question, also involving emotions, images and so on, are different from the apparent ones. In order to function without the burdens of our minds and bodies, it is essential to become convinced of the primacy of the animic over the corporal, in the generation of our ills. Mental sanity is a primacy for our rational behavior. To have this clearly established, it must be emphasized that there are considerable pains and sicknesses that are not recognized by our being, simply because they are not perceived (the nervous system does not send the signal to the brain). This suggests that frequently some of our problems can be eliminated by disregarding them. Illnesses that illustrate this outcome are as common as bad breath, allergic reactions, and a cold. Equally as our brain is the key for recognizing these ills, it also can display an extraordinary curative power, as illustrated by the automatic generation of some enkephalins such as dopamine and endorphins, into the organism. These considerations do not negate the existence of many illnesses of more strictly corporate or physiological origin, but even in these instances, the power of the mind (and even more of the spirit), palliative effects and cures can be attained.

But the essence of what we have just explained, is that *mens sana* is the most important part of the saying. And because of it, it behooves us to make evident the way in which our mental, emotional, and imaginative mechanisms, bring about a conundrum of irrationalities which determine mental unbalances, and a posteriori, our physiological and psychological infirmities.

It is necessary to recognize that the process of biased thoughts and emotions which follow the multiple stimuli that we experience every second of our existence, and which are based in superficial beliefs that are not compatible with the essential and central ones that constitute the nucleus of our beliefs and our essence, lead to actions that generate the mental and corporal infirmities that we suffer. We should be continuously and constantly vigilant of this process as to avoid continued stumbles that complicate and limit our life, impeding it from reaching plenitude. In doing so, we would only be reinforcing our natural tendencies, given that our mind, when it functions normally, is continuously debating these fundamental ideas, not giving in to irrationalities in most instances. Nevertheless, many other times panic attacks take hold of us, or processes of negation (or acceptances), habits, compulsiveness, or obsession, etc. lead to behaving in a sickly way.

F) Additional Treatments

Many times, to get rid of this baggage of irrationality which limits our productiveness and impedes the happiness that is offered to us in this world (if we reference our life to the design of the Creator (God). We must start by establishing certain corporal behavior. It is well known that behaving in a habitual way generally derives in an acceptable mental scheme. Sometimes this schematic behavior is broken when our behavior is contrary to it. The repetition, by a decision imposed by our will, of certain corporal behavior, even if our mind is not convinced of them, can lead to breaking down certain irrationalities controlled by our frontal cerebral lobes.

It must be recognized that the above is based on the non-separability of body and soul, with the mind being part of the former. *A fortiori* if it is understood that the brain and the rest of the body are not separate compartments. Therefore, an alternative way of working out these problems, even though it would depend on the specific case, is in finding the solution to our ills in the mind and the brain, through the elimination of the biases in the collectivity of thoughts, emotions and images that circumstantially influence our behavior. This route is quicker and to the point, but it may have to be reinforced by proper corporal behavior.

Take for example the case of alcoholism. Even though we fully understand how customary behavior a la Skinner is created, and we know all the set of biased thoughts that lead us to repeat "one more drink and then no more", or "never will I be able to kick this problem that I have inherited", and set us for a fall, nothing will be accomplished if we do not force our body to restrain from imbibing for the next four hours. Without an act of willpower, determining our corporal behavior through which we deny ourselves the possibility of walking to the closest liquor store (or to the place where we hid the bottle), it may be insufficient an analysis of all the traps laid out by our mind when we see a beer advertisement on television (stimulus) which lead us to a syllogism of biased, emotions and thoughts whose only conclusion is that we must zip some alcohol. The counter corporal habit of quietly remaining in this place in which we are at, and refraining from looking for a bottle of alcohol, could be quite useful to be liberated from being a drunkard, and similar habits (like gambling).

G) Mental Exercises and the Body

Our mind and the rest of the body are closely united within the same physiological and corporal structure. The brain is the origin of the nervous systems that every millisecond controls the various functions of our organism. Therefore, if we want to attain control over our extremities, our heart, our lungs, etc., our mind can accomplish it. That is, mind and body constitute interactive mechanisms. Both hypnosis and biological feedback have been techniques that have strongly shown this to be the case.

The same can be said about the human soul in its relationship with both our mind and our body. Here, the key resides on faith and will, which are the mechanisms that put to work the very powerful and supernatural spiritual powers. The communication channels are pristine because of the grace received from the Lord with respect to the primacy of the spirit over matter. Without referring to the miracles, there are numerous examples of these attributes of humankind, which allow dominion over pain and illness, the facing of the worse of tragedies, suffer the most intense pain, and undertake prodigious feats, all by spiritual power. Medicine is aware of these forces, and frequently uses them by the intelligent use of the placebo effect.

The secret of success in the accomplishments just mentioned is repetition, so as to develop receptors in the brain cells that make them an acquired behavior. At the same time, this repetition creates the confidence that our mind and brain can accomplish them. Concurrently these abilities are developed so that we attain the assurance that these mechanisms are under our control. These are the fundamental characteristics for the success of human beings in any task, and they define what training experience and capability in anything tried from an early age can accomplish, and how eventually we can become professional in our performance.

H) Physical Exercises and the Psyches

Many mysteries of human life cannot be explained, but certainly it is known that physical exercise creates a positive reaction in the organism, including the mind. It makes us feel inwardly and outwardly healthier. Only recently have we been considering the scientific hypothesis about how exercise can have these effects, without it being presently shown to be false.

The psychological effect of exercise is equally strong. And it has not been refuted presently. After we exercise, even though we might be physically tired, a feeling of mental fulfillment is achieved, which could be related to an extra-corporal effect, like the satisfaction of having accomplished a task or the fulfilling of a plan of action. But perhaps the fundamental explanation is what we have referred somewhat above, which is the influence of the coma (soma) over the psychic through the intercommunicating links between them.

It is known that the body and the brain are linked through all the corporal systems, like the the nervous and the circulatory ones. This gave rise to the term psychosomatic, which derives from the Greek word just written above. It is usually thought that it flows from the mind to the rest of our organism, but it also operates in the opposite direction. Equally, we tend to forget the corporal influence over mind and spirit, but among other things, remember that physical work has been considered an essential part of the ideal of perfection that are and were sought by the Catholic monastic orders.

I) Summary and Conclusions

Humans must fight against numerous afflictions and physical and mental symptoms. Many of them are automatically repressed by our organisms, whether because there are limits to the amount of information we can process, or generally, by the limits of our rationality. Others are prevented from reaching consciousness especially during infancy and early adolescence, because they cannot be confronted appropriately. Those that reach in our consciousness are mostly perishable, as they will be promptly replaced by subsequent ones. Sometimes, however, we fall into the trap of worrying about them, or giving them importance under the vein of defending the ego. In this way we provide them with permanence in our conscience, and we excessively worry about them. Furthermore, in certain cases we offer them the possibility of irrupting into our consciousness, and even in an obsessive-compulsive manner, thus creating a habit. This unfortunate path should and could be avoided.

In confronting these problems, we can count on a powerful ally in the essence of our being, where our deep convictions lie, which is known to control our will power, exercising a powerful influence over our behavior. This center of goodness that we can also call spirit or soul, is framed in the image and resemblance of our Creator. The functions of our mind and nervous system, are mostly influenced by the essence of our being which, even though confronted with numerous thoughts and emotions, constitutes a pilot that leads us to safe port, because it guides our actions, which is the fundamental part of our behavior.

For the treatment of the psychological and physiological problems of humankind, this spirit constitutes a powerful ally. From controlling blood pressure to confronting prejudiced and negative thoughts based on passing impressions that pummel us, these are the fundamental objectives of the famous motto: *mens sana in corpore sano*. Even when bodily actions lead to changing mental attitudes, as when repeated corporal actions break the habit of certain phobias or panics, the initial force, if well examined, resides in willpower which expresses, our essential beliefs.

VII

LOVE, WORK AND HAPPINESS

A) Happiness is an Indirect Occurrence

Love is the principal source of happiness. But curiosily is attained by loving, and not by its direct pursuit. When one offers love, psychological plenitude is obtained. Why is this the case? First, because we realize that within us, we have something that has value, and we feel fulfilled in giving it to others. Remember that we cannot give what we do not have. Furthermore, according to Carl Gustav Jung, only by giving it away can we know that we have it. Second, not only does our self-esteem grow when we give of ourselves to others because we have something that they value, but also because we perceive that the love given to others signifies that we love ourselves, which is the source of this richness of love that we have accumulated, and that voluntarily we pass on to our neighbor. If we hated, or were indifferent to ourselves, we could not love others, because it would not be inside us. Third, many times our love is requited, which is an additional source of happiness, especially when it is unexpected, or when we do not make its retribution a condition.

Not only is happiness a sub-product of love, especially if it is unconditional, but it is also a consequence of the work that is done. Remember the saying by Sigmund Freud that life is just love and work. These lead to the aliveness of human beings and lead them to attain total fullness. To fill joy in working, as we frequently feel when we have finished an arduous job, make us co-participants in the work of creation, which is continually developing. Nothing is created or destroyed in the universe, but it is only transformed, according to the first law of thermodynamics. This means helping ourselves and others, because we indirectly produce all that sustains our lives, and partially those of our brothers. In it and because of it, work is indissolubly tied to love. Finally, to be able to contribute through our work means that we can exercise our qualities, expressed in the ability to work, to produce something that others appreciate, which makes us surer of ourselves, as it underscores our attributes.

Thus, it is through love and work that we attain happiness, notwithstanding the circularity of its fashion. If we try to attain it directly as a bullet, we shall destroy the possibility of its achievement, because it results from the things we do, and it results from such an exchange. It should be noted that it is not only happiness that has such characteristics in our lives. There are many goals that if pursued with great intensity are not attained, because they make us tense and overly conscious. These span from sport activities to intellectual pursuits, covering a wide terrain in between.

B) Happiness Starts with Self-Acceptance - Esteem - Love

It should be explained that the love we have within us has its origin in the acceptance of ourselves. If we did not accept ourselves, we would not like what we are, which would lead us to internal struggles and clashes which would generate unlove. If we do not love ourselves the way we were created and have developed, we could not generate love. Thus, the importance of having faith in the existence of a God that loves us, as this cures all internal conflicts and harmonizes the human being with himself, which is essential for the rest of creation to move within love, which is the essence of what He is, because without his presence, everything would tend towards destruction.

On the other hand, acceptance of ourselves is the road that leads, through love, to value the way we are, and slowly improve ourselves. If we love ourselves, we also have self-esteem, and these two we transmit to others. And we generally receive it back! What bigger happiness we could feel than what all of this produces indirectly!

C) Only if We are Happy Can We Transmit Happiness.

And when we transmit happiness, we become happy ourselves. As has been explained in previous sections of this chapter, not only happiness, but all that has value in this world, involves a bypass, which implies that all that has value and can be enjoyed results from a process that is mostly indirect. Another of the important applications of this principle is that, to cure and help ourselves, the best way to attain it is through our efforts addressed to help and cure others. We establish in our concentration in our neighbors, the capacity to cure and help ourselves (nobody gives what he does not have). Moreover, the self-realization impelled by our efforts with our brothers will further strengthen the internal attributes that are given to others. It is well known that those who teach learn the most (*docendo discimus*). Finally, the recognition and thankfulness that we receive from our neighbor, and the recompense from our help, will further aid in curing ourselves.

The same occurs with happiness. We can only give what we possess. In the case of happiness, the same principle that applies to love, knowledge, confidence and secureness, faith, etc., is even more evident. A happy person makes others want to be happy as well. As happens with alacrity and joy. But note that the receptor must want to receive the donation for it to be trespassed.

Furthermore, as happiness is passed on, it renders towards those that originally have generated it. As our brother receives happiness, and reproduces it, this increase returns to us. Which makes us even happier, even though we were its original source. And the better we do it, by incarnating ourselves into our neighbor, it returns to us engrossed and more effective, as if it were the others, and not us, that generated it. We should always keep in mind, of course, that the happiness that is passed onwards, is indirectly regenerated, as we have explained it at the beginning of the chapter.

D) Work and Love Foster Other Orientation

As pointed out in a previous chapter, the approach that is most conducive to mental serenity and balance is directing our life following our internal direction and orienting it towards others. When we behave lovingly, this is what we are doing. The love that we pour from the interiority of our being, we direct it towards our neighbor, sharing it with him. Thus, love finds its reason for being in our fellow neighbor, reinforcing the sense for a balanced life, which mostly means an orientation towards others.

The same can be said of work. It is something that constitutes a decision of our will. And even though it might appear that it results from egotism, if closely examined, we work with and for others. We give our potential energy, to help the advance of humanity, and to put our talents to produce for others. It is not done as much to sustain ourselves, which has been shown to represent a small fraction of the emoluments received, but to make us useful. To give sense to our lives. And our self-esteem grows as we find that others accept our efforts, and recompense them by efforts of their own. This is why one of the great costs, in terms of welfare, that humans suffer, takes place when the gifts that our Creator has donated to us cannot be put to work through long-term unemployment. The psychological impact of unemployment represents perhaps the major part of this economic phenomena.

But we must emphasize that both love and work must be directed by our most central and essential beliefs, accented by our faith, and hardened by our will. If not, there would be the risk that we would lose ourselves in innumerable acts of labor and love without purpose, that would be put forth with no sense at all. The principal example of the kind of life that we should follow is the example of Jesus who, while giving love and working for others, never lost sight of the establishment of his message, even while living entirely free and without an agenda. Remember all the time he devoted to prayer, fasting, penance and reflection, inspired by his faith in following the designs of the Father. In the gospels we find continuous references that Christ would leave the masses that followed Him with which He worked and which He loved (especially the apostles and other disciples) to concentrate in the basic purpose of His mission, to ensure that it would direct His actions.

E) Love and Work Avoid Self-Consciousness

As directed toward others, love and work help us distract ourselves from excessive inward preoccupation which is the source of anxiety and anguish. These latter ones draw us apart from the happiness we attain when we concentrate ourselves on our fellow or other, orienting ourselves towards them by our own validation and decision. In finding ourselves in our neighbor, they find ourselves in us, and give back the love and effort that we have given them as neighbors. All this, of course, begins with our own self-esteem and love, and in taking care of ourselves, because again, we cannot give what we do not have. But when this self-love leads us to an incommensurate growth of our ego (egotism), we worry so much about our welfare, and so little of that of others, that we build a proclivity towards the worrying and analyzing of our self, and become too conscious of our thoughts and behavior, which lead us away from happiness, not to say our mental and emotional balance.

This tendency to be fundamentally conscious of ourselves, and of what is happening at every moment, imprisons us into a downward spiral of observation and analysis of ourselves, which limits perception, judgment and acting in the social world. We feel oppressed in ever more concentric and narrow circles, which increasingly center on oneself. Worrying about how we are performing and what is happening to us, is only tinged by our own selfishness and intellectualities, and we cannot escape from our own traps, to perceive the outside world and judge from its perspective. As a consequence of this, we develop a perfectionism which leads us to request from ourselves behavior and actions beyond our capabilities, and to be continuously measuring and judging them, following standards that are not only unattainable, but also wrong. All this ends up imprisoning our mind in a detention center where the light of day, which is outside ourselves, does not reach, and that we ourselves block because of a set of prejudiced thoughts, derived from excessive self-examination, egocentrism, and personal follow-up, which infringes upon natural behavior. We lack the self-confidence that we can only attain in the last instance from the faith that in our interior we have in God, and which explains to us what we are and the value we have in the place we occupy in Creation.

The best antidote against an egotistic, obsessive-compulsive, and hypochondriac scheme, is to forget ourselves. For that purpose, we surrender to the needs of others; we live for our neighbor; we concentrate on our brother. Curiously, this constitutes the Christian doctrine. The cognitive-emotional or behavioral therapists of today cure their patients with the ideas of Jesus Christ, which teach not only how the Kingdom of God can be attained, not only in Heaven, but also on this Earth.

VIII

ACCEPTING AND CHANGING

A) Acceptance Of Spontaneous Events (including Thoughts and Emotions)

Human beings are all different, but at the same time, they are the same in about 98 percent of their characteristics or attributes as defined by biology. Each person has the value that his or her Creator implants, and it is thus infinite. There are not superior or inferior beings, because we are created with identical values. As we all have a conscience which leads us to evaluate ourselves and our actions, this super-ego tends to judge us too harshly. Because of it, on many occasions we do not accept our behavior. Our emotions, our weaknesses, our behavior, bother us so much that we declare war on them in our minds. But as has been explained in previous chapters, the more we try to erase an idea from our mind, the more it remains and becomes present. Paradoxically, only if these are accepted as something typical of our being, can we then change them.

If we devote ourselves to frontally combatting them, the bother that they produce will increase and we will increasingly become aware of them. And the mental receptors that alert us about the things that bother us, will immediately prepare their reactions. The first and most powerful of which is doubt and/or worry. This could be followed by somatic and psychological reactions, but the first response is sufficiently strong as to ensure that these bothersome symptoms appear with certain frequency in our conscience, because as we worry about them, we concede them an uncommon importance.

This is why, even though it might appear contradictory, the more we accept ourselves, the easier it will be to change. Of course, this implies that as an act and decision of our will we want to modify something which is not going well in ourselves. But the path begins by recognizing what we are before changing and integrating and loving it as an enemy that we have inside, and that we are going to convince ourselves that it must change. Yet it will only be accomplished by replacing bad behavior with good actions. We must concentrate on strengthening what is good, and not on debilitating what is bad. The latter will not be attained (as happiness), little by little, after the loving acceptance of our defects, and the willingness for change, which is effectively realized in our actions.

B) The Non-Acceptance of Negative Behavior (including Habits and Actions)

When we do not accept our thoughts and emotions, they will reproduce, return, and grow. Thus, the worrisome behavior will be maintained because of our worry. Many years ago, many more than I would like to remember, I attended a movie theater which showed only cartoons. The one that impressed me the most had to do with Donald Duck, who was supposed to be the best friend of Mickey Mouse. Donald was in bed at night to slumber the evening away. Everything seemed to be going right until the Duck became aware of the noise made by a drop of water as it fell from the pipe to the wash basin in his bathroom. The drop of water came down with regularity every few seconds, and innocently ran through the spigot towards its destination outside the house. But the faint noise bothered Donald, and consequently he could not fall asleep. Instead of accepting the slight disturbing noise, regularly produced, and not worrying about it, which would certainly subdue him into the hands of Morpheus, the God of sleep, he tried to suppress it. First, he covered his ears in countless ways. Next, he tried many times to fix the leak. Finally, totally frustrated, he wrestled with the water main and forged a momentous outpour of water that inundated his home. His inflexible and obsessive-compulsive reaction not only failed to take care of the original drip-drop, but made the leak much bigger. Of course, he could not sleep or do anything else the rest of the night, save to fight against a monster that he himself created by his lack of acceptance Accepting the original drip-drop and shifting his attention span to the relaxation and pleasure of sleeping in his accommodating bed, or else allowed his mind to flutter from one vision to another, he would have accepted the drop of water, relegating it out of his conscience eventually by consuetudinary forgetfulness.

This experience foretells that to remove a negative thought or emotion, the best we can do is to let it be, accept it, and not to worry about it, render it important, or concede it an audience. Using the tactic of not confronting it and trying to change the thought, but rather continuing with what we were doing without trying to change our ideas and emotions, especially if they are positive and agreeable, the negativity will disappear by itself. Not accepting perpetuates the negative behavior because we want to force our way.

Our mind is, generally, a changing one, and it is difficult for any thought or emotion to last but for a few seconds. As is well known, it is very difficult to concentrate. In addition, our willpower allows us to choose what we want to pay attention to, and even when we are affected by worry, hypochondria, obsession, or compulsion about something. Our will always allow us to overpower the negative experiences and finish what we are accomplishing, while the negative distractions eventually disappear.

Consider that frequently we have temptations that come to us from obscene or grinch-like thoughts, and hateful or envious sentiments. Not only Christianism but also Buddhism, consider that these temptations are uncontrollable and that they constitute thoughts and emotions that attack our minds (temptations), but that can be changed by thinking of something else. We should not be frightened or be brought down by them, but consider that they are normal expressions of our self after original sin, and that we can "erase" them from our consciousness with the help of our will, by concentrating our thinking on other matters. Saint Teresa of Avila wrote: "Nothing should worry you; nothing should frighten you; everything moves on, God does not move, and patience prevails. He who has God lacks nothing, only God suffices." And she also used to say that imagination was the crazy guest we housed in our self.

C The More We Accept, the More We Change

This is like magic. Nobody would believe it unless we explain it in terms of love. It happens that when we have the will to change, but we are not at peace with ourselves, even to the extreme of displeasing ourselves, the absence of love will be like a ladder that ties us to our past (the same happens when we want to help others). But accepting ourselves is loving ourselves. And love dominates the importance of the behaviors we want to change, so that they vanish without even us paying attention. Even though it is possible that now and then our old habits resurrect, or that they remain in our unconsciousness and rise on certain occasions.

The first thing an alcoholic or a drug-user must do to get rid of their addiction is to accept that one has it. With that acceptance comes, as we have written before, the recovery of self-worth, throug loving ourselves as a being created with intrinsic value. That way he reaches the recognition that his worth is as great as that of any other human being, whose individuality is different from that of others, and impossible to clone, and whose singularity makes our presence in history not only important, but also inexplicable. Only then can we understand that our will can mold what we accept we are. (In the same fashion that God accepts and loves us as we are, but ask us to improve through love). And that is how the typical alcoholic or drug user begins to travel the road to a life without drugs or alcohol, knowing that his desires to consume will return to bother, because they had become habitual, but being certain that they could be defeated day-by-day, on the basis of the will power to do other things. On these truths, is the treatment of alcoholism and drug abuse based, as established worldwide by Alcoholic Anonymous. The first step is to say: "I am an alcoholic," or "I am a drug user."

Looking at it from another standpoint, the self-acceptance we recommend, emphasizes a distinction among thoughts, emotions, remembrances, phobias, compulsions, obsessions, anxieties and angsts that devolve in the mental milieu, and the actions which represent the most serious and permanent manifestations of what we want to accept (and what we are) because they involve our willpower. But the first, when they constitute profound beliefs, are the origin of the latter, and must be given priority. All these manifestations of the mind are very complex and complicated. And they could be called cheaters and trappers, by trying to erode the essence of our beings. However, what we initially must learn through the process of acceptance is to not be scared of them, nor to give them undue, importance because they only reside in our minds. Afterwards, it must be understood, that even though they appear to sabotage us (affirming, for example, that really, we could not accept what we wish to) they do not have any power to do so because of "free will," and that they even help. Because they make us aware of danger, and of our own weaknesses (this is why we must even accept the thoughts that we should not accept). Consequently, it is necessary to make them our friends, and even to laugh about them, which would not be an obstacle to change, but rather would facilitate it, if our will shall decide and execute.

D) Acceptance Means Disappearance; Rejection Means Expansion

Human nature must be accepted as it is. Without giving it much hought, it is widely accepted as part of the popular folklore, such expressions like "do not give it a thought" (do not waste time on it), which were used in Cuba, my country of birth. We never pondered whether this saying made sense or not, but rather followed it verbatim. And informally we found out that those who did not follow this advice did not do well. These traditions that had been decanted by decades, perhaps coming from Spain or West Africa, were drops of wisdom. And they represented simplification decanted by centuries of experience about what we have been examining. If we do not resist the things that come to our mind without opposing them, they will depart on their own. But if we insist on eradicating or examining them, for one reason or another, they will stay with us longer than they should be fostered by the attention we afford them.

Even though we are conscious of the thoughts and emotions that we have on many occasions, that is, we are aware of their existence, they tend to always be spontaneous. Frequently they catch us by surprise. And most of the time they follow one another, with some of them being subconscious. With those we should begin to practice acceptance. If we cannot accept our own thoughts, much less will we be able to accept our habits, behaviors, and performances. To justify that we should focus on them, frequently we tell ourselves that these thoughts tend to be crazy (which comes from popular folklore). Thus, this view also comes about from our social customs, and even our own instinctive experience. Little by little we start to understand which of these thoughts and emotions we should pay attention to. And with maturity, some that used to torment us, are now accepted, and thus made to disappear. We accept nightmares and infantile dreads, shifting our attention to other matters. But if rejected, which implies fighting them, affording them attentive audience, giving them attention, assigning importance to them, and worrying, then they can become phobias, compulsions, and obsessions, which is equivalent to following an infantile behavior with respect to them.

However, some get upset with unexpected emotions or negative thoughts, or at least some of them. For example, those who desire total control of everything related to self, or that tend to be perfectionists, reject these irrational thoughts. They consider them dangerous, or that they imply imperfections. Unfortunately, they do not realize that what is problematic is not having them, but worrying about them, which could turn into an obsession, compulsion, or phobia. For this type of individual, it is better to obtain acceptance of these thoughts and emotions, realizing that they all have a positive purpose, as they alert us of dangerous or difficult situations, which require us to act carefully. In other words, we imagine the problems we may have to face, to be sure they are avoided. And on other occasions we become conscious of our thoughts (accompanied by emotions) when they are irrational and negative, in order to prevent their influence over our behavior.

E) By Stressing the Positive, We Convert and Reduce the Negative

As we have just written, if we capture the purpose of irrational thoughts, we can evaluate them in a different fashion. In this way, what appeared negative could be turned into positive. Anyhow, the judgement of a thought as positive or negative is internally accomplished, *through a value judgment* which unfortunately is often time hidden in the subconscious or unconscious, unless we decide to rescue them from their anonymous existence and force them out into our conscience.

In principle, we must emphasize that everything that reaches our mind could have a positive purpose. Beginning with the fact that emotional thoughts that are not based on reasoning are part of our human condition, that even though we ignore them, they surely offer, altogether, a positive balance of the good and the bad. We should not become our own *deus ex machina* and try to proudly remake ourselves as we would like. We should not forget that the greatest temptations form the greatest saints, and that those do not become sinful if are accepted for what they are, and we do not voluntarily enter into the actions and imagining that they suggest.

From the above we generate the idea that everything has a positive side. In reality, this is a philosophical posture based on recognizing willpower in sublimating the negative thoughts that suggest: "I cannot." Even though as has been seen in the previous paragraph, it is not required to reach this posture, the same is sufficient to ensure the effacing of the irrational thoughts. And it emphasizes that willpower in the end imposes itself, and that in the end it represents an arbitrary decision of saying yes, of selecting and affirming our beliefs. Of course, some people would do it with greater ease, because of their character, by not allowing themselves to be scared by these ideas, or their repetitiveness, while others would have greater difficulty as they are more doubting and impressionable, but every one can transform what appear to be failure into success.

F) Emphasizing the Positive we convert and reduce the negative

As we have previously written, acceptance is another mechanism that leads us to success. And in any case, the two methods can be combined. Remember that when we do not accept negative thoughts, it is implied that the vacuum has to be filled with positive ones, and thus the original ones will disappear from focus. Our posture, there-fore, should be to continuously introduce positive thoughts in our mind and behavior, and the first one is the acceptance of the negative vibes that reach us.

The same thing happens with the change in others. If a person with whom we have intimacy bothers us with their attitudes, the worst thing that can be done is to reject her because of that. In that fashion we will never lead her to change, as our rejection will lead to a similar reaction on her part. However, if we accept the behavior, it will surely catch her attention, probably leading the other person to consider changing the attitude on her own, always on the basis of accepting oneself. If this is accomplished within a climate of love, as has been pointed out above, the greater the chance of success. Why would acceptance produce such remarkable change? Because it must come from the love we give to ourselves or to others.

There have been many that have popularized these ideas, which originated in rational-emotive and cognitive schools. They emphasize that our mind has "erroneous zones," as Dyer would say. We are continuously bombarded with these thoughts, emotions, sentiments, images, etc., and they should be accepted for what they are, knowing that they can only be affected by them if we give them an audience. In their place we must voluntarily introduce thoughts, emotions, images, etc., that are positive or rational while we let the others be (accepting them). Thus, the negative or irrational thoughts, emotions and images should be left alone (accepted), knowing that their sources are our erroneous zones.[24] Finally, we must make clear that such acceptance implies a series of thoughts that are subsumed in the sub-conscious and that tells us: remember that these are irrational emotions that should not be rebuked, but rather accepted as such. But subsequently add rationality and concentrate on rational thoughts and emotions.

G) The Stimuli That We Generate and Receive (A)

In the next paragraphs we will follow what Dr. Albert Ellis called, in his early books of the end of the 1950s and the beginning of the 1960s, the rational-emotive theory. In a more simplified fashion, this author later characterized it as the ABC theory, thus the letter with which we begin this section, placing it in parenthesis.

Suddenly, a negative thought arrives in our mind and coupled with it an irrational and emotive feeling (that is a biased thought). For example, we have just bought a new car, but there are a few problems tied to the acquisition. Immediately, a feeling of anguish and sorrow afflicts us. These are the stimuli. We should explain that many people frequently experience the feeling or emotion without relating it to how it is tied with the thought that preceded it. Only those observant and conscious persons are aware of such mental behavior, become aware of their relationship. In other instances, the stimuli come from outside us. For example, we must cross a steep path. We become aware that it is close, and consequently a frightful sensation takes hold be us, which may even cause panic. We feel the impression that we are going to plunge below and die, although we are conscious that all this is produced by phobia that height has generated. We think that we will lose control and plunge into the abyss.

---

[24] Dyer even applies these concepts to hypochondria and even the early symptoms of sicknesses, which he affirms do not affect them, because of his concentration in the positive, and inattentions to the negative.

H) Beliefs and Insights, Deep and Superficial, Guide the Interpretation of the Stimuli (B)

A stream of thoughts and emotions, produced or biased, follow the stimulus as wagons following a locomotive.[25] Remember that an emotion is a biased thought. We are aware of some, while not of others, because these are incorporated in the fog of the subconscious, thus being more dangerous. These constitute the reactions that Albert Ellis implies under clause B of his psychological analysis of neurosis, today dismembered into several families of mental problems, like obsessions, compulsions, anxieties, phobias, panics, paranoias, etc. At this moment, the person experiencing the reactions to the stimulus may allow itself to be overcome by this string of biased thoughts which constitute false beliefs, or could instead appeal to his internal beliefs that reside in the essential nucleus of his existence. It is important to point out that frequently, this process takes place intuitively, instinctively, or unconsciously, and the person is not aware of what is happening. It should also be clarified that when we remit ourselves to an essential belief, this has sufficient power to dismember and demerit the string of emotions that affect us, and to clearly prevail over them.

Now and then, when these beliefs surface as a thought, or sometimes as a string of them, disarming the emotional reaction based on irrational beliefs, when we first have the stimulus. Is required on other occasions those positive reactions emerging from our beliefs, which erase the negative ones, do not come forth, but instead a thought is produced that reinforces our basic essences and tendencies, and makes clear that the negative ideas stand against what we intrinsically believe, and thus could not be true.

---

[25] This perception is owed to Ramón Boza, M.D., Professor of Psychiatry at the University of Miami, and member of the V.A. Hospital medical staff in the city of Miami.

I) Reactions to Stimuli Become more Rational ©

The behavior that ensues the stimulus and that constitutes the last step in the quick chain of happenings, we represent by a capital letter C. Whether the stimulus is automatically produced, or it has an outside source, if we allow ourselves to be taken over by negativity, irrationality or emotion, the final behavior influenced or intermediated by irrational beliefs and the negative images that accompany them, will end in generating actions that are counter-productive to the person. For example, if the stimulus consists in forgetting about something which we think we should remember, while we partake in a friendly reunion, and a series of irrational thoughts ensue leading to the conclusion that we have Alzheimer's disease, immediately our behavior would lead towards inhibition, which would inhibit us from participating in the ensuing conviviality.

From another angle, if the final reactions to the stimulus are tied to the recognition of the mediation produced by a series of irrational thoughts and reactions, we will be able to unmask their negativity, and make the intermediate step B a rational process that brings about consistent with rationality. In the example just mentioned in the previous paragraph, if as we become temporarily oblivious of unforgettable things and consider the series of irrational beliefs that we have been ruminating for some time, which tend to assure us that Alzheimer's has set in instead of an appeal to rationality takes hold, the final reaction (C) will follow another path. Under the latter circumstances we would become aware of how common these slips of memory arise and how extreme is to conclude, led by a panic reaction, that we have been seriously affected by the feared disease. Therefore, the action that rationally would ensue is to ignore the worrisome stimulus and to continue to actively participate in the meeting. It should also be stated that worrying about Alzheimer's disease will make us prone to forgetfulness, which will tend to provide a false confirmation that we have been afflicted by the sickness.

Generally, our actions are the result of the forces embattled in instances A and B. If we have perceptions of our erroneous thoughts, and we accept them, without following them, we can understand our natural tendencies towards irrationality (intrinsic in human beings) and direct our actions towards healthy mental processes. And even though we do not understand fully what is happening in a perceptive and clear way, our instinctive tendencies, and our basic and deep beliefs, make us aware that we should not allow ourselves to be impressed by irrational thoughts, and that our willpower dictates that we should behave in a rational way, discarding false neurotic beliefs. This is a way our behavior ends up being more rational than we think, imaging or emote.

J) Motivation and Will Power as Key

To overcome all the problems described in this chapter, the most powerful forces that we can count on our favor are willpower and motivation. The latter really is one of the prompts of the former, but we want to expressly mention it because it has been concluded that without it subjugating habits and compulsion reducing them to unimportance is very difficult. On many occasions it has been found that individuals that cannot overcome these abnormalities, have not seriously decided to change. They are not willing to exercise willpower, to abandon the roads already trite of alcoholism, agoraphobia, idleness etc., through the efforts of knowledge and control of oneself that they require.

At the same time, it is necessary to recognize certain limitations of willpower. In the same way that we cannot entirely control nature, since we are part of it, we cannot entirely control ourselves. That is why we should be aware that after we have controlled habits and compulsions, they tend to recur as natural tendencies to continuously return to these unhealthy habits. It would be idyllic to think that we can control with our will what comes into our mind, and that we should expect the recurrence of the negative forces already considered, as well as negative thoughts, denials, repressions, and cognitive dissonances. They will accompany us to the end of our lives. But our willpower can impede that we recur in weakening in the face of these negativities, and to behave in accordance with them, further than their inevitable and unimportant presence of them in our minds.

As has been pointed out already, worriedness about negative thoughts which lead to negative emotions, brings them into focus and allows their disarming. The same can be said about those related to compulsions, unhealthy habits, obsessions, and other facts of human neurosis, which make us conscious of what our minds are brewing when they emerge into consciousness. If they remain hidden in our subconscious, we cannot easily recognize them, and when this happens, they can influence our behavior more readily.

Worriedness is one of the ways in which we rescue them from the apparent anonymity that they maintain in our senses. This is why our perception of them empowers us to bring them into awareness and allows their disarming (the same goes for denial, repression, and cognitive dissonances), as long as we do not worry excessively about them. By becoming conscious of the mental tendencies that could influence us, more easily can they be neutralized by appealing to reason and common sense, and to prevent that, unsuspectedly, they would influence our actions.

IX

THE CONSCIOUSNESS OF THE UNCONSCIOUS

A) Revealing the Unconscious: The Layers and Density of Thought

"Well read and written" individuals often even professionals in psychology, in numerous instances consider that the subconscious of humans, and even more strongly their unconsciousness, remain hidden to individuals. Nothing further from the truth. When the one-time tennis champion Martina Navratilova showed a certain facial expression, her trainer, who had psychological training, as is commonly the case in sports, could describe accurately the string of thoughts, supposedly in an unconscious manner, that went through her mind. She later confirmed, after an auto-examination, that it was the case. But not only Martina, but any other person could have done it on their own. This amounts to going from the unconscious, to the subconscious, to the conscious.

We must recognize that we are obviously referring to two levels. One is the most hidden: the unconscious. With the subconscious, without much effort, we obtain a vague notion of the thoughts that bother us. The unconscious is most submerged in us, and a detective's effort is needed in getting to know them. But we must distinguish between the unconscious and those supposedly repressed from our infancy, which require the greatest effort to recognize and define them, whether by a psychologist or psychoanalyst. Yet, even on most occasions, even this achievement is within our reach, if we make a strong, concerted, and repeated introspective effort.

How is it that we discover the subconscious and the unconscious? It is by analyzing our actions that represents the most direct and easy way of ascertaining them. Additionally, your emotions and your thoughts could ascertain them. If we are aware of our salivating while not looking at or smelling a succulent dish, it can be interpreted as if we have remembered one. Equally in the just examined case of Martina Navratilova and her facial expressions, tied to her sub or unconscious thoughts, from our salivating we can bring to light the memory of a dish that we had tasted and then liked. Equally a thought or emotion if we retrospectively follow it, its leads will bring us to mental forces initially hidden, that determined or produced them.

B) The Power of the Subconscious and Unconscious to influence our Actions is Limited

In reality, our actions are determined by immediate and rational forces most of the time. It is true that on some occasions, emotive forces of an explosive nature predominate and turn off our reasoning. But what hides in our subconscious is kept at the level of dreams and fantasies; of what we would like to have but cannot attain. Exemplia gratia: our image of making fun of the boss does not become reality. Today, psychologists and psychiatrists that deal with obsessive-compulsive disorders, are able to correct them in months, attacking the proximate cause of these phobias, without attacking them like olden times by the erroneous ways that were in vogue when the psychoanalysts tried to discover the sub-consciousness in their pristine and/or past origin.

By knowing the actions that we are undertaking, because of our unconscious and subconscious, we can confront our (C) in the Ellis mechanisms without having to examine the circumstances that activate them. For that we only must examine the circumstances that activate them (A). For that we only have to carefully examine our systems of beliefs, expressed through our thoughts and emotions, which constitute the (B) as defined by Ellis.

Using repeatedly and frequently this method, it becomes second nature, so that it is spontaneously followed, it becomes natural, and we apply it spontaneously. We note, by our actions and emotions, that something irrational is influencing us. As Dyer has pointed out, we become aware and understand that these origins arise form the erroneous zones in our minds, or as Father Anthony De Mello, S.J. would have commented, from the desires that sprout from our weak human nature (fear, egotism, unlove, etc.) We ignore them by affirming our belief, that there is nothing that could force us to act or feel by mistakes of reason or negativity.

C) Imagination and Dreams (Day and Night)

Most thoughts and emotions generated by our organism are like dreams that we have when awake. The mechanism that creates them is our imagination. Daydreaming is a succession of images that place us in hypothetical situations that we construct with the objective of experimenting with alternative scenarios. Even though we are not close to knowing with some precision why these are part of human nature, it cannot be doubted that they detract from our person, in fact it can be argued to the contrary.

It is known that the dreams we have while sleeping have important purposes. They come to be during one of the stages of sleep, when our eyes are rapidly moving. During these relatively short periods in which our dreams are intensified, our brains are fixating on our brain memories, everything that has happened in the day that preceded, making it more easily available to our remembrance. Through dreaming, we also go over our daily experiences in a symbolic form and prevent difficult situations that we will have to confront.

The dreams that we call daydreaming, in which our imagination practices to make us conscious of possible mistakes, is a way of preventing they will occur. We daydream about dangers that we may have to face, while considering the situations that a person could face soon, experiencing at the same time sporadic sensations of nervousness, and even fear. All this resembles the dreams experienced when we have rapid eye movements, or dreams, or REM dreams.

D) Recognizing the Contributions of Negative Thoughts

We all have negative or irrational thoughts. There are three classes of them, depending on our consciousness: unconscious, subconscious, or conscious. The first thing that must be recognized is that the latter are the most useful to prevent dangers or difficult situations that we might have to overcome. The subconscious ones, and even more the unconscious ones, are much more difficult to control, in terms of the influences that they could have over our behavior.

If we do not become aware of their usefulness, and alternatively are frightened by them, and consider them presages of what would happen to us, we will give them undue attention. Which would be equivalent to thinking that they represent reality, and that our thoughts are real life occurrences. If so, we would be misinterpreting thoughts that only exist in our minds, and that only constitute an efficacious mechanism of imaginative defense.

Even if well interpreted, these irrational and emotional thoughts, thus negative ones, we realize *that they make us aware of the danger* of being impressed by them and even being suggestible to them, or establishing a complex because of them. Having a bit of scenic fright and nervousness before public speaking should be considered normal preparation, before the event, which prompts the adrenalin to flow. Worrying about them makes us aware of the danger of giving importance to the symptoms, so that we would not fall into that trap. As Father Juan B. Cortes, Ph.D. in Psychology from Harvard University and at one time Chairman of the Department of Psychology of Georgetown University used to say in his classes, "nobody has ever died for not sleeping but it would be possible for this to happen because of continuously worrying about the possibility."

E) Changing the Unconscious through Positive Thoughts

As has been written before, when negative or emotional thoughts attack us by assault, it is best not to combat them directly, but rather to use our willpower to concentrate on positive or rational thoughts and actions. The more we allow ourselves to be hurt or molested by negative thoughts, sentiments, or feelings, the more difficult it will be to get rid of them. Therefore, as Father Ignacio Larrañaga has written, "we must become friends of these emotional thoughts, and even welcome them." Or how Father Cortés, S.J. used to say, "laugh at them" (and I say with them). When we are not entirely aware of them, it is more difficult to realize their presence, but they can be identified by their negative consequences, and then change all the irrational scheme through the establishments in our being of thoughts, emotions, and actions that are rational or positive.

All this is very easily said and written, but would it not be difficult to accomplish it? The "open sesame" is to be aware of the power of will and of faith, acting through our mind. The free will with which we have been conceived allows us to choose between one thing or the other. When we choose the positive one, and fix our awareness on it, the other eventually become forgotten. Choosing rationality in our actions, thoughts, and emotions in these situations, we would increasingly cleanse our subconscious and unconscious mind of their negative thoughts and emotions, and the irrational behavior they suggest, even if they repeat themselves in the short run. When they do, we should recognize their quality of making us aware of them, and the dangers that they might imply, instead of remaining in the unconscious and the subconscious, where they would be more difficult to contend with. As Father Larrañaga would say, "befriend them," or Father Cortés would suggest, "count with them and laugh them off". Our free will allows us to disregard them, while recognizing how they help in making us aware of their existence, and realizing they help us combat those that are subconscious or unconscious, through rational thoughts and decisions. In this fashion, our mental and corporal achievements would improve, through the recognition that these thoughts and emotions should be disregarded. As Dr. Wayne W. Dyer states, "they are part of your erroneous zones, and should only be recognized to alert you of them." In his famous book *The Feeling Good Handbook*, psychiatrist David D. Burns, Clinical Professor at Stanford University, now Emeritus, alerts us of the process of *fear*, generally defined by psychologists and psychiatrists as "false evidence appearing real," and stresses that these thoughts and emotions should be disregarded.

Generating more positive thoughts improves mental performance, as do conscious commands. Positive directed commands to the unconscious can turn it around. It must be understood that irrationality in the unconscious and sub-conscious spear a reaction that helps us become much more rational. Thus, the usefulness of even the negative thoughts and emotions by making us aware of the danger they pose. It must be known that they originate from ancestral times, when humans faced a more dangerous existence, and needed to be aware of these dangers in order to fly or fight. If we do not allow the fright, panic, or nervous paralysis that this syndrome could bring about, by worrying about it, we should count on them as reactions that even today can help us.

F) The Foolishness of Fighting Negative Feelings and Emotions

It is childlike as we have just stated in the previous section, to fight negative emotions and feelings, that as has been made clear, are none other than irrational thoughts. They have to be experienced because they warn us about problems. And then they vanish unless we allow ourselves to be annoyed or worried by them. Why could this happen? Because our brain is unconcentrated by nature and numerous stimuli assault every second. Because of which they disappear on their own, if we do not insist on putting them under microscopic mental examination.

It also happens that irrational thoughts frequently come from our past experiences. They constitute doubts of our adequate behavior in the past, to which we have previously responded, but these answers do not instantly come back to our conscience which if they did, they would not remain in our conscience. If we insist on immediately having an adequate comprehension of what engages in the stimulus in question and begin to analyze it in a "perfectionist" fashion, it will only result in retaining the erroneous thought, because giving importance to all thoughts or worries is equivalent to combatting them.

Finally, it is necessary to acknowledge that human beings cannot control what enters their mind. The best that can be attained is to concentrate your mind on the positive and rational ones. Furthermore, it must be assumed that our Creator allows them for our good, like he allowed that his saints suffer the most egregious tests, so that they would be molded through temptations. It must be clear that negative and irrational thoughts are like temptations. Faith and willpower are tempered by tribulation.

X

CONCLUSSIONS

A) A Good Essence

Our beliefs, B in the rational and emotive theory of Dr. Albert Ellis, the letter meaning "beliefs" in English, have a deep and profound existence in our minds. Thus, they are not affected by irrational thoughts and negative emotions. These just pass by, and when we appeal to the will of our rationality, and to solid and immutable beliefs, we reaffirm the latter. Negativity and irrationality, like temptations, challenge our essence, which is characterized by good wisdom, and most of the time are repelled right away.

It is important to observe that when we are not rational in our thinking, the original biased phase (A) quite frequently is replaced by irrational one. If we examine it, this curious behavior demonstrates that frequently we are not conscious of the second thought, that is negative, which is tied to the previous one, that usually affirms: "the first irrational thought is really the truth, and you should adapt your actions to it, or at least worry, and rethink things, to determine what you are really convinced of."

On certain occasions negative thoughts and emotions make us think that our beliefs are not those that truthfully exist in our nucleus of good sense. These irrationalities, that even as we have explained before are flashes of unreality, and thus should not have importance, are still dangerous, because they could confuse or impress us if we give them attention. Thus, we should exercise caution and be aware that they can arise whether they are hidden in our subconscious or not, even though they are ephemeral and unreal.

If we award importance to these irrational ideas, it amounts to giving them life and permanence. Then, instead of being like dreaming while awake, they become part of our reality, because we are providing them with an audience. If we do, they could paradoxically become important, as during a given period, they could blind the clear perception of our system of beliefs that constitutes the essence of our being. This occurs through the string of irrational thoughts that follow the first, that has been given reality and fixation in our mind.

B) Nurtured by Faith and Confidence

If we pay attention to emotions and thoughts that are negative, and we worry about them, whether by recognizing them when becoming aware, or intuitively by the negative sentiments that they compel, this could affect our actions and behavior. Therefore, we should not give them importance because of the potential changes that they hold (even though they do not have a permanent and real existence). And if they hold this presence for a longer time, take flight from them.

Self-confidence is important for our attainment. And this is why we must be constantly connected with the essence of our being, where our real and deep beliefs are fixed. This is why we should not allow irrational thoughts to cloud the mirror in which we see ourselves as we really are. Therefore, when the heated water of emotions harbors an image which is tainted, we must immediately recover our true vision of what we are, through the cold water of indifference and reason.

Self-confidence arises from our good, rational, and positive essence, where our beliefs exist. It is based on faith, because we must assume the value of the human creature, which extends to ourselves. Our self-value is evident, because we exist, having been created. This is the original starting point of all we are and have. Our values stem not only from what we are, but also because the rest of reality truly exists, and we perceive it though our senses. If not, we would not know of the existence of something outside of ourselves.

C) If God did not Exist, We Would Have To Invent Him

It is impossible to give what we do not have. That is why, in order to believe, learn and know, it is essential to have confidence in oneself. If we do not have it, we cannot believe in anything, because we must have faith in ourselves. If we do not have it, we cannot believe in anything, because if we do not have faith in ourselves, it is impossible to have faith in something. The same can be said about learning to know. If we do not believe in ourselves, how can we be sure that we are learning or finding out what is true?

Doubt and faith are present in everything, and most importantly in science and religion. Doubt serves as a reaffirmation of our self-confidence, as temptation reaffirms our intention to remain free of sin. Doubts are really like negative thoughts that we have seen can help us to take flight from dangerous situations, or to prepare us for better accomplishments. In the ultimate instance, from the smaller to the larger questions, are resolved in terms of faith.

Without a creator it is difficult to understand our existence. Moreover, it is more improbable to think of a process of auto-generation for the whole universe, or inclusively they minimally required matter needed for the Big Bang. As it is rational to assume we have been created. That effort already gives us value, especially because nothing that we know has been created, has the ability of self-creation without DNA. This dignifies our existence, because of the life that was given to us, we infer the confidence that we must have in ourselves to have faith and understand everything that surrounds us. Faith in ourselves is intrinsically ours, because genetically and instinctively, it becomes intuitive. As the programming through which all other animals rule their behavior. But all of this does not rule out that we have doubts, and that they extend even to our intrinsic value.

D) What is Instinctive and Learned

If what we have previously expressed were amply known, human beings would not have the proven tendency to feel inferior. This latter trait is an intimate one, as the vast majority overpower this instinct most of the time. Probably contributing to our inferiority complex, the immensity of creation, and the feeling of smallness that we harbor within it. As we must transmit to every person that is born, all that is outside of our instincts, that is, transmit to them through direct and indirect teaching, all of the cumulative knowledge of the human species. Most of this requires our *faith* in that we can accomplish things that an infant feels are rather difficult, as their conscience awakens, such as reading.

Something that we learn early at school, in addition to confidence and faith, is that we have willpower. Intuitively, it is what made it possible that we could first move on our own, make sounds imitating language, walk, talk and not defecate but in our pampers. There is something even more mysterious that we have discovered and that comes from our Creator: the love that God felt for us when He made the Creation possible and our participation in it.

Apart from our instincts, what conditions us is what we learn, that also makes possible the development in ourselves of the capabilities that prepare us for life. But to make this possible it is necessary to learn based on faith, the accumulated knowledge and the will that convinces us. Thus, to believe in anything is something that only immediately requires of our volition to accomplish it. Some doubt the existence of the historical figure of Christ, but believe that Hannibal, the Carthaginian crossed the Alps with a herd of domesticated elephants, of which there is much less evidence.

E) We are What we Do

The capability of humans to accomplish things further above what has been genetically inherited, and which has been stamped in our instincts, depends of our faith and willpower as we go through the process of learning from the inheritance of knowledge that our forerunners gifted us, and afterwards from the formation of habits that are bestowed by our repetitive behavior. This repetition brings consequently, that the things we have learned to do, will eventually become instinctive in ourselves, that is they become second nature, and that they do not require that we must be careful, nature, and that they do not require that we must be careful, pay attention or make an effort to accomplish them. As Karl Popper and Richard Eccles wrote in "*The Self and Its Brain*," learning makes them automatic.

All human beings confront a series of atavistic behaviors that complicate our effectiveness in our actions, thoughts, reactions, etc. These really constitute warning signs and worries about our efficiency, that if understood and made by us, could even have beneficial effects. We must recognize that similarly to dreams (while sleeping or awake), they constitute part of the normal reconsiderations that humans have, and which have been developed as part of the evolutionary process. What must be clear is that many of these thoughts (or emotions, images, etc.), whether conscious or unconscious, are only part of reality as they exist in our minds. Yet in essence, they are not part of what exists outside of ourselves, or even of our internal truths. And only these latter ones should guide our decisions and behavior.

Contrastingly, actions are part of reality, and this is why they are imbued of rational thoughts and positive emotions and sentiments. The latter, like rationality, are the ones that foster our well-being, making us feel better, achieve success, experience greater happiness, etc. We could let our thoughts derive to irrationality without any danger, we can let them freely drive to experiment emotions and feelings without anguish, as long as they only exist within ourselves, but not in external or internal realities. When it is about reality, and the consequences it brings, we cannot afford the luxury of negativism or irrationality, and then we behave in accordance with what we really believe.

F) Liberty and Willpower

We can choose what we want to do and believe, but not our thoughts, stimuli and emotions that erupt in our mind. However, as free will has been given to us, as well as willpower, we have the discretion of directing our attention to the sentiments, images, and thoughts that we are concerned with, or turn away from those in which we are not interested or that could perturb or harm us. Also, we have the power to concentrate on those matters that appear to be beneficial or attractive to us.

Will power that God has given us is powerful. It allows us to reject the most powerful temptations. Control the most unrestrainable emotions. Overcome the deepest sentiments, overpower the most powerful tendencies coming from our conservation instinct. Undertake unimaginable heroic feats. Withhold extraordinarily painful sufferings. Sacrifice ourselves for human solidarity and act heroically in serving lofty ideals. Our powers of concentration gifted to us, allows day after day of work, forgetting our more basic desires (hunger, sleep, etc.) in order to reach our goal.

That is why, when using our free will, we can modify our behavior, and channel our thoughts and emotions, to serving the attainment of a defined objective. Therefore, we firmly believe that when a person expresses that a harmful behavior cannot be changed, it is because he does not want to or does not know how. This book has provided various indications of what is the essence and how to overcome this whirlpool, and of the ways in which we can take advantage of irrationalities and incandescent negativisms (that is, that do not stay in our mind because concentration is hard, or because they are replaced by different ones) to be in the alert of failures or potential dangers.

G) Lieben, Arbeiten and Happiness

Love (Lieben) means acceptance. As soon as we begin accepting us, we will begin to love ourselves. If we were disgusted with what we are and what we do, we could not love ourselves because we would be desiring our change, which is an unconformity with what we are at the present. This does not mean that we will never want to correct our defects. But the first and most effective path to accomplish this, is to know that we accept ourselves, which implies that we know and love ourselves.

As we have previously said, life implies not only love (Lieben) but work (Arbeiten). These take us to happiness if we embrace them fully and live them wholly. To offer love to others it is essential that we love ourselves (and therefore accept ourselves). As Karl Jung wrote, it is not possible to give what we do not have. Lao Tse also said that if we only look to ourselves, we do not illuminate; as we give to others, we illuminate them and also ourselves. If in our interiority we do not breathe a loving attitude for what we are and live, we cannot in any way transmit it to others. Remember that we cannot give what we do not have. If we do not love ourselves, we would not know how, nor we could love our neighbor (as we love ourselves).

When Freud wrote in the latter way Lieben und Arbeiten, what constitutes living and how it could mean happiness, if we define it in this quite effortless way, it was most difficult to accept that work is pleasurable. But even an existentialist writer like Baudelaire exclaimed: Il faut travailler, sinon par gout, au moins par desespoir, puisque tout bien verified, travailler est moans ennuyeux que s'amuser. (We must work, if not by liking it, at least by desperation, because if everything is well verified, working is less tedious than having fun). Moreover, if we carefully think about why work mortifies us, we understand that mortification is a conditioned reflex based on an arbitrary definition that we have adopted. But if we question the process, we are made aware that we are accepting as true an irrational thought. As soon as we confront this negative emotion against work, that molest us, we can evaluate it as what it really represents and is, a vital activity from which we can always derive contributions, and that objectively we can even like. Contrast these interpretations with those that characterize those that make a dominant habit of work (workaholics) which make a similar error by definition and lack of reasoning at the other extreme.

H) Accepting Shame, Guilt, Shyness, Fear, Anxiety, Panic and Other Negativisms

All these tendencies are, more or less, natural in human beings (we are not referring, of course to the mentally ill). Those that have them more often are the precocious. Those that have them more often are less cautious. The latter tend to be less successful in life in the medium and long term. Therefore, we should befriend all these emotions and irrationalities. It is only when we worry about them, that we consider them as enmity, and we reject them, that they tend to grow in us in an abnormal way. If we accept them, they could not have a negative influence over ourselves. Remember that feeling inferior is being human. Before the enormity of God and his creation, it is rational to have these sentiments. The other animals that are led by instinct do not feel either inferior or superior, because they live instinctively. They do not suffer or enjoy these negativisms and irrationalities that humans have, because they do not have free will, willpower and reasoning.

To man, these negativities should not surprise them, because they mean paradoxically, that we can understand our position in the universe. We are aware of our dependency but at the same time, we recognize our superiority when compared with the animals, because we can change, even if infinitesimally, the world, given our freedom. But at the same we are creatures and not creators, and because of that, dependent on our Creator. Because of all of this, being conscious of the negativisms implicit in our existence becomes positive. When we count on them, they cannot surprise or hurt us.

I) Never to Worry, Never to Rate, Never to Doubt

Worryness is the Achilles heel of human beings. The thoughts that continuously pass through our mind are passing experiences. Many of them are accompanied by images and emotions that are negative. But knowing the typical imagination of men and women, many of them are allowed through without consequence. However, if something worries us it remains trapped in our conscience. Then we begin to consider and reconsider it and it is possible that other negativeness allied to the first will accompany it. All the above could become an increasingly worrisome chain of irrationality, which progressively increases our degree of worries, until it unfurls in an extreme case, in panic, mental paralysis and even a neurosis crisis. The best way to stop this mechanism is willpower, and with the convincing belief that the above is a common process that occurs when we allow ourselves to be impressed, inhibited, self-suggested or feel insecure with something. Faithfully believing in the previous analysis, we stop the worrisome string of negativisms abruptly, without allowing ourselves to ponder or speculate further about it. The worst that could be done is to try reasoning during this process because we are affected by nervousness or combatting it frontally on the base of trying to erase the thoughts and emotions that these strategies are affecting our with mind.

J) From the Unconscious to the Subconscious, to the Conscious

Extremes should be avoided ("virtus in medio est"), according to one of the basic conclusions of human wisdom. In everyday living, while we are doing things and simultaneously perceiving experiences, we should not either ignore them completely, or fixate our attention on them. Rather, we should keep ourselves vaguely and mildly aware of what is happening to us, to be able to take corrective measures when required. But at the same time not over rationalizing the stimuli that we perceive, reacting in a compulsive-obsessive way, and making them the focus of our thoughts.

Our conscious mind can manage simultaneously about seven thoughts in the mediate memory. Through which we can be vaguely conscious of various matters, although we are mostly concentrating on two or three. Our capacity to accomplish multiple chores concurrently is something that we adapted from our mind, when we invented computers. And to do so we do not need large efforts because it is part of our nature, and we can accomplish it in a relaxed fashion. Of course, at any moment we would be concentrating on a particular thought to be efficient in our accomplishments. But this does not impede us from being occupied in keeping the other balls (physical or mental activities) in the air, as good scramblers.

Finally, we must understand and be convinced that unconscious and subconscious ideas are within the clouds of mystery. They can be recovered at any moment by exercising our memory and reasoning in a certain way. The way to do it is to focus our attention on the last emotion or thought we have become aware of and follow it upstream to both the original stream of thought. Little by little we will discover original thoughts and emotions which stringed together, gave rise to the string of sensations that brings us to the present. We are not insisting that this process is easy to accomplish, but that it is possible for any man or woman that is patient, who have a reasonable memory and a certain curious spirit. On the other hand, the incentive to bring it about is large, because they will discover how our arbitrary thoughts and emotions determine our behavior and given the negativity and irrationality that commonly prevails in our minds, we will have an ample margin to improve our behavior.

With this last and powerful concept, we finish the summary and conclusions about the ideas exposed in this monograph. We have seen that human welfare can be attained in this world, but it is brought about not by matter, but through the spiritual approach, in which all of us are rich. It is worthwhile to finish by recognizing the perfect happiness of Jesus while in his Sacrifice because he was redeeming us. It is the other (the neighbor), as his example indicated, which fully fills us with happiness and makes us worthy. Another way in which to practice what this book conveys is to follow the example of Jesus Christ.

XI

SYNTHESIS OF THIS BOOK

I. INTRODUCTION

A) Objectives of book
1. Psychological Welfare
2. Philosophical Outlook
3. Role of Faith

B) Nature of the book
1. Thinking, Introspection and Reading
2. Review of Major Psychological Pitfalls
3. "The Art of Living": Principal Issues

C) Scope of the book
1. Limits to Knowledge
2. Self Help
3. Source of Problems is Mental

D) Review of book coverage

E) Acknowledgements

II THE MEANING OF LIFE

A) The Mystery
1. Spaceship Earth
2. Existential Needs: A Transcendental Explanation
3. Scarcity and Rationality

B) Questioning: The Universe and the Molecule
1. Bohr and Plank vs. Einstein

2. Anthropomorphism
3. Dimensions for the spirit

C) The Spirit, the Mind, and the Body
    1. Different but Interrelated
    2. Parts of the Whole
    3. Primacy of the Sprit
D) Lieben and Arbeiten
    1.Continuous Worry
    2.Simultaneous Thoughts, Emotions, Singing
    3.Love and Work

E) Transcendental Urgings and the Resting Place
    1. Who and where are we?
    2. Attracted to the Supernatural
    3. What is our Destiny?

F) Living as an Art
    1. Life is an art (a trick) that should not be questioned or answered.
    2. Living should just happen immanently.
    3. When is psychotherapy needed?

G) Inner Direction
    1. Self-worth, self-esteem, self-respect
    2. Self-reliance, self-confidence, faith
    3. Self-direction and free will

H) Other Orientation
    1 To serve oneself is to serve others.
    2 Serving others
    3 Being loved and being served

I) Recapitulating
    1. The Mystery unfolds through oneself
    2. Serving and doing and realizing what one is

III   BEHAVIOR: NATURE OR NURTURE

A) Human Potential (Immanent knowledge, etc.)
    1. Fetal Behavior
    2. Infant Behavior
    3. Early Conditioning

B) Human Limitations
(Impressionability, etc.)
    1. Wiring Pitfalls
    2. Myopia
    3. Repression

C) Ensuring positive net results (II,2) (II, 4)
    1. Cognitive Dissonance (denial) and its Avoidance
    2. Rational-Emotive Behavior
    3. Solution orientation

D) Differences with Animal Instincts
    1. Conscience
    2. Consciousness
    3. Free Will

E) Instinct, Intuition and Reason
    1. Genetic Influence
    2. Intuition and Common Sense (sense that we have in common)

F) The Basic Faith required for Living
1. Accepting knowledge
2. Other Basic Assumptions
3. Self-confidence as Key
(we give what we have)

G) Handed-down Knowledge
1. From generation to generation
2. Message subtly passed from
infancy on
3. Generally available knowledge on
Life

H) Acculturation from early-on (through school and social interaction)
1. Role of the family
2. Role of the School
3. Role of the Peer groups

I) How Strong a Force is Acculturation
1. Strong but not as much as instinct
2. Shows how to live more fully
3. The Passing of the torch

J) Custom, Habit, and Behavior
1. Social Customs
2. How Custom and Habit Determine
Behavior

K) Do People Really Modify their Behavior?
1. Yes, with Willpower
2. But the Flesh is Weak
3. Main Traits more Difficult

L) Summing Up: How much does one know; How much does one learn?
1. Genetic Endowment
2. Knowledge Accumulation
3. Behavior Repetition

IV.   THOUGHT, EMOTION, IMAGINATION AND BEHAVIOR

A) Straight Line Relation or Interaction
1. Both
2. As we think, we imagine; as we imagine we emote.
3. As we emote, we behave.

B) What is Thought?
1. Electro-Chemical Impulses
2. Strings of Concepts
3. A Process stringing words (thoughts) to get there

C) What is Emotion?
1. Biased thoughts
2.   Pregnant with Feelings and Images
3. Full of Value Judgment

D) What is Prejudiced or Biased Thought?
1.   A thought that rates and judges
2. (A thought) tinted by a certain proclivity
3. (A thought) that assumes, many times unknowing.

E) What is the Role of Imaging?
1. A reaction to a sensory perception

2. Precipitating further reaction or action
3. Mostly images of Pain or Pleasure

F) To what extent all of the above influences behavior?
    1. Unless thwarted by a contrary image, yes
    2. Images of positive or negative nature extinguish each other frequently

G) Does Behavior influence all of the above?
    1. Behaving influences the above
    2. Actions behoove thoughts.
    3. Actions change biases, emotions and images.

H) Thoughts: rational and irrational
    1. Both
    2. Beliefs generally rational
    3. The usefulness of both

I) How do you know?
    1. Intuitively
    2. Experience   Partly reason
    3 What works better.

J) Are Emotions, Negative or Positive?
    1. Both
    2. Depends on the Results
    3. More difficult to control than thought.

K) What is important as a measure of positiveness and rationality is our behavior
    1. The ultimate outcome of all forces are the action vector.
    2. They shall be known for their deeds

3. All others exist only in the mind.

L) The Spiritual Mind and its deep rooted Beliefs.Ultimately Control Behavior

1. Our beliefs tend to be

(II-3), (II-2)   impervious to thoughts,

(II-2)   emotions, biases, images, etc.

2. Spiritual Power determines Behavior.
3. Relation between Spirit and Beliefs

V. FREE WILL, WILL POWER, AND FAITH

A) The Choosy Chosen: Exceptions of Free Will?
1. Predestination
2. Behavior Modification
3. The Addictive Person

B) Destiny and Change: Challenges to Free Will
1, Limited Options
2. Genetic Predisposition
3. Behavioral Determinants

C) How much can People Change?
1. Break habits.
2. Control emotions
3. Work to Change

D) Possunt qua posse videntur
1. They can because they see themselves do-ing it.
2. Repetition makes for confidence.
3. Faith, Self-Confidence, and Convincement

E) Faith, Self-Confidence and Convincement

1. For self-confidence you need faith and vice-versa
2. Confidence allows a realistic self examination.
3. Confidence allows being yourself.

F) The Interactions of Faith and Willpower

1. To change you must be aware of what you do.
2. With self-confidence you can change what you do.
3. With will power you can change what you do.

G) Acceptance, uncertainty, and change

1. Acceptance and change
2. Accepting Uncertainty
3. Change by stressing the positive

H) Self-confidence and Knowledge

1. Deep down beliefs are stable (thoughts)
2. Superficial thoughts (beliefs) are unstable.
3. Faith in yourself is essential for beliefs

I) The Role of Doubt

1. Required to discover truth.
2. Does not compromise knowledge, faith, or confidence.
3. Belief is established from doubts.

VI. MENS SANA IN CORPORE SANO

A) Brain, Body, and Mind: Interaction

1. Each influences the other
2. But the Key is in the mind

3.. The Mind is a guiding mechanism

B) Psychosomatic Manifestations
   1. When the Ego affects the brain
   2. When the Super-ego affects the brain.
   3 Discarding the Freudian Id

C) More Strictly Physiological Problems
   1 Sickness is caused by the subconscious or un-conscious.
   2. Anxiety and physiological ills
   3. Depression and physiological ills

D) More Strictly Psychological Problems
   1. Psychological Ills caused by neurosis.
   2. Psychological Ills caused by Obsession-compulsion.
   3. Psychological problems caused by anxiety, fear and insecurity.

E) Treatment of these problems
   1. Awareness of the causative thought processes (with emotions, images, etc.)
   2. Realizing the nature of irrational thoughts, and how to dismiss them.
   3. Understanding and parsing the processes of thoughts and beliefs.

F) Additional Treatments
   1. Treating the Body and the Brain
   2. Treating the Mind and the Brain
   3 Combining the two above

G) Mental Exercises and the Body
   1. Brain communicating to the body

2. Mind communicating to brain and body.
3 Repetition, confidence, control and skill

H) Physical Exercises and the Psychic
    1. Exercise and Mental health.
    2. The psychological impact of fitness
    3. Exercise and body-brain communication link-ages.

I) Summary and Conclusions
    1. Body and Mental symptoms, worrying and repressed thoughts.
    2. Interactions among Mind, Brain and Body
    3. Treatments of Physiological and Psychological problems.

VII. LOVE, WORK, AND HAPPINESS

A) Happiness is an indirect occurrence.
    1. Psychological plenitude is in loving others.
    2. Happiness is a by-product of love and work.
    3. Happiness cannot be pursued.

B) Happiness Starts with Self-acceptance-Esteem-Love
    1 Love as Acceptance
    2. Self-worth and Happiness

C) Only by being happy can one Transmit it and Vice versa
    1. Only by helping others can one help oneself.
    2. Transmitting happiness
    3. Happiness rebounds

D) Work and Love foster other Orientation.
    1. By loving we abet other orientation.
    2. Work has similar qualities.

3. Work and love should also be self (or inner) directed.

E) Love and work to avoid self-consciousness.
1. Self-consciousness can lead to excessive analysis.
2. Concentric patterns of analysis and worry are dead ends.
3. Love and work drive us away from them.

VIII.   ACCEPTING AND CHANGING

A) Acceptance of spontaneous events (including thoughts and emotions)
1. The more we accept ourselves, the more we change.
2. The more we fight thoughts, the more they bother us.
3. Things that bother us grow in importance unless we ignore them.

B) The non-acceptance of negative behavior (including habits and actions)
1. Not accepting perpetuates the behavior because of worry.
2. Not accepting perpetuates the behavior because we want our ways.
3. Not accepting perpetuates the behavior because what we oppose grows.

C) The more we accept, the more we change.
1. We have to accept even the thoughts of not accepting.
2. We have to learn to laugh at our negative behavior (habit action thought)

    3. This does not mean that deep down we will not work for change.

D) Acceptance means Disappearance; Rejection means. Expansion.
    1. We have to accept human nature as it is.
    2. Thoughts are spontaneous even though controlled.
    3. Negative thoughts are in the end positive, as they have a purpose.

E) By stressing and converting to Positive, we reduce the Negative
    1. Changing the negative into positive
    2. Turning failures into successes
    3. Stressing a positive approach and positive thinking.

F) This applies to others as well
    1. Do not try to erase the negative, but to introduce the positive.
    2. People are converted as well.
    3. Our acceptance transforms them.

G) Self-generated Stimuli have meaning (A)
    1. Like negative thoughts
    2. Like emotions
    3. Like fear and panic

H) Deep and superficial insights guide Interpretations of stimuli (B)
    1. String of negative superficial insights might ensue.
    2. Just one positive, superficial insight might counter.
    3. If deep insights are positive, as usual, they would prevail.

I) Reactions to Stimuli become more Rational (C)

    1 Actions that result are more rational than thoughts.

    2. Stimuli are guided by the insights into the reactions.

    3. You can parse your insights to make them realistic and rational.

J) Motivation and willpower as key.

    1. Motivation and will power will eliminate important compulsion and reduce them to unimportant.

    2. Worriedness about negative thoughts brings them to consciousness. and allows their disarming.

    3. The same goes for denial, repression and cognitive. dissonance.

IX   THE CONSCIOUSNESS OF THE UNCONSCIOUS

A) Unveiling the Unconscious: the layers and density of thought

    1. There is really nothing you cannot bring to consciousness, if you work at it.

    2. The subconscious is less hidden than the unconscious

    3. From your actions, your emotions and your thoughts you discover the sub and uncocious.

B) Realizing the limited Power of the Unconscious to affect actions

    1. Unconscious and subconscious thoughts have limited impact, and none when noticed.

    2. By being aware of their influence, we can thwart them without knowing them

3. With willpower we can ask our mind to sub
   and unconsciously do the above.

C) Imagination and Dreaming (night and day)
   1. Most thoughts and emotions are like dreams
      during daytime.
   2. Like dreams at night, such dreaming during
      the day has a purpose.
   3. They usually are acting out or going through
      motions for improved performance.

D) Being Aware of the Contributions of negative thoughts
   1. By being aware of them we guard against their
      influence.
   2. By having them we are warning ourselves of
      dangers
   3. Some of these are the dangers of being scared
      of these thoughts.

E) Changing the Unconscious through positive thoughts
   1. Generating more positive thoughts improves
      mental performance.
   2. Conscious commands can improve perfor-
      mance.
   3. Positive directed commands to the uncons-
      cious can turn it around.

F) The foolishness of fighting negative feelings and emotions
   1. These negative thoughts entice us into positive
      actions.
   2. They constitute the remnants of flight or fight.
   3. You cannot control which thoughts come to
      your mind.

X   SUMMARY AND CONCLUSIONS

A) A good core

1. Our beliefs lie deep down inside, hidden by confusing thoughts and emotions.
2. Hidden and evaluative negative thoughts and emotions sometimes drive us to think that our beliefs are otherwise.
3. If we give importance to, or even consider these, negative thoughts form out, driving the core into a bad period.

B) Nurtured by faith or confidence.

1. If we fall prey to bad suggestive thoughts, our performance is impaired.
2. Self-confidence is essential to accomplish things well.
3. If it is based on faith, since we assume our self worth, which is self-evident and the starting point of everything, we have and are.

C) If God did not exist, we would have to invent Him

1. We believe, learn and know based on our self-confidence, because we cannot give what we do not have.
2. Doubt and faith come together in science and religion.
3. A Creator is intrinsic to human existence.

D) The instinctive imprint and learned behavior.

1. We have as human beings, largely by instinct, and following passed-on knowledge. This is all we need to perform well in this world.
2. Through faith and will power we can expand our accomplishments as if mutating

      3. Apart from instincts, we are conditioned through learning which builds skills akin to instinct.

E) We are what we do.

      1. By repetition and eventually habits, we build deep beliefs that we can do things.

      2. Thoughts are part of reality, but their essence is not.

      3. Actions are part of reality.

F) Freedom and Willpower

      1. We can choose what to do and what to think.

      2. God has given us a powerful will.

      3. Thus, we can change.

G) The Bottom line on Positive and Negative thoughts

      1. Positive thinking improves performance.

      2. Negative thoughts can be changed into positive thoughts

      3. Everybody has these thoughts, and they can be handled without problem.

H) Lieben, Arbeiten and Happiness

      1. Love means acceptance and can bring change.

      2. We have to love ourselves to love others. We cannot give what we do not have.

      3. Work can bring happiness, if you give it a chance.

I) Accepting shame, guilt, shyness, fear, anxiety, panic and other negativisms

      1 Being friends with your negativisms

      2. Feeling inferior is being human.

    3. Awareness of negativism is good; not to be surprised by them.

J) Never to worry, never to rate, never to doubt
    1. Worry creates strings of negativism and even pain.
    2. Analyzing brought by doubt is as fruitless as a final proof is elusive.
    3. Rating ourselves (alone or through the rating of others) creates worry and doubt artificially.

K) From the unconscious to the subconscious, to the conscious
    1. Both extremes, being conscious or unconscious over matters, can and should be avoided.
    2, In the immediate memory we can carry at least seven thoughts at the same time, some can do several things at once, and we can concentrate on those we chose.
    3. The unconscious and subconscious can always be brought to mind, by retractive our thoughts and emotions.

LIBROS PUBLICADOS EN LA COLECCIÓN FÉLIX VARELA EDICIONES UNIVERSAL SINCE 1965

Published books of Christian-Cuban thought

01) 815-2   MEMORIAS DE JESÚS DE NAZARET, José Paulos /1996/
(La vida de Jesús bellamente contada en forma de memorias)

02) 833-0   CUBA: HISTORIA DE LA EDUCACIÓN CATÓLICA 1582-1961
(2 vols.), Teresa Fernández Soneira /1997/
(Historia de las órdenes religiosas que se dedicaron a la educación en Cuba y de todos los colegios religiosos que existieron en la Isla.)

03) 842-X   EL HABANERO, Félix Varela (con estudio de José M. Hernández e introducción por Mons. Agustín Román) /1997/

04) 867-5   MENSAJERO DE LA PAZ Y LA ESPERANZA
Juan Pablo II
(Documentos y homilías de la visita de Su Santidad Juan Pablo II a Cuba) /1998/

05) 871-3   LA SONRISA DISIDENTE (Itinerario de una conversión), Dora Amador /1998/
Artículos sobre Cuba, la disidencia y reflexiones sobre la vida de hoy y la conversión al cristianismo y al servicio religioso.)

06) 885-3   MI CRUZ LLENA DE ROSAS (Cartas a Sandra, mi hija enferma)
(3ª edición ampliada y revisada), Xiomara J. Pagés /2001/

07) 888-8   UNA PIZCA DE SAL I, Xiomara J. Pagés /1999/
(Artículos y reflexiones cristianas sobre la vida de hoy)

08) 892-6   SECTAS, CULTOS Y SINCRETISMOS, Juan J. Sosa /1999/
(El autor es sacerdote católico y en este libro estudia algunos movimientos religiosos que influyen a familias hispánicas en USA., incluyendo la santería cubana.)

www.ingramcontent.com/pod-product-compliance
Lightning Source LLC
Chambersburg PA
CBHW031129020426
42333CB00012B/292